DYNAMICS OF STRENGTH TRAINING

Gary Moran
Professor, University of San Francisco

George McGlynn
Professor, University of San Francisco

  Wm. C. Brown Publishers

Book Team

Editor *Chris Rogers*
Developmental Editor *Cindy Kuhrasch*
Production Coordinator *Peggy Selle*

Wm. C. Brown Publishers

President *G. Franklin Lewis*
Vice President, Publisher *George Wm. Bergquist*
Vice President, Publisher *Thomas E. Doran*
Vice President, Operations and Production *Beverly Kolz*
National Sales Manager *Virginia S. Moffat*
Advertising Manager *Ann M. Knepper*
Marketing Manager *Kathy Law Laube*
Production Editorial Manager *Colleen A. Yonda*
Production Editorial Manager *Julie A. Kennedy*
Publishing Services Manager *Karen J. Slaght*
Manager of Visuals and Design *Faye M. Schilling*

Consulting Editor
Physical Education
Aileene Lockhart
Texas Women's University

Sports and Fitness Series
Evaluation Materials Editor
Jane A. Mott
Texas Women's University

Cover photo by Bob Coyle

Cover design by Jeanne Marie Regan

The credits section for this book begins on page 154, and is considered
an extension of the copyright page.

Library of Congress Catalog Card Number: 89–60404

ISBN 0–697–07638–5

Printed in the United States of America by Wm. C. Brown Publishers,
2460 Kerper Boulevard, Dubuque, IA 52001

10 9 8 7 6 5 4 3 2

Contents

Preface

In the past few years there has been a rapid advancement in scientific research relating to muscle strength and endurance. In addition a myriad of new and innovative strength training devices and techniques have been introduced. As a result it is virtually impossible for the average individual to distinguish between what is valid and safe from that which is false and dangerous. The purpose of this book is to give clarity to this new information by providing a simple, logical and individualized approach to strength and endurance training. The book also is intended to be a practical guide for understanding the physiological basis of muscle strength and endurance and the most efficient and effective strength training techniques. The information presented here represents a consensus of presently available scientific evidence.

This book attempts to bridge the gap between scientific knowledge and the application of that knowledge and also to provide you with the most efficient and up to date methods of strength training to insure that your body's adaptations from the training are beneficial and safe. How to select and prepare for physical training and understanding how the exercise affects you physically over both short and long time periods of exercise are also basic questions that are answered in this book.

A sequence of simple tests enables you to evaluate not only your present muscle strength and endurance but also your cardiorespiratory endurance, body density and flexibility. The first part of the book describes the benefits of strength training, basic fundamentals and exercises, motivational and mental concentration techniques, and muscle training procedures. Other important areas covered are cardiorespiratory endurance, strength training for women, injuries, nutrition, drugs and an analysis of various strength training equipment. The text also provides record sheets and profiles for tracking your strength and endurance level changes.

This text is intended primarily for college physical fitness classes, strength and weight classes, circuit training, and body building.

Introduction

1

Objectives

After studying this chapter you should be able to:

1. Describe some of the misconceptions concerning strength training.
2. Describe the physiological benefits of strength training.
3. Describe the psychological benefits of strength training.
4. Describe the body's adaptation to strength training.
5. Define body building.
6. Define muscle endurance.
7. Define muscle power.
8. Define muscle strength.
9. Define weight lifting.
10. Define power lifting.
11. Define weight training.

Importance of Strength Training

Little doubt remains today as to the importance of muscular strength and endurance in competitive sports and in the demands of everyday physical activities. Whether you are an athlete looking for increased performance, a sedentary individual dissatisfied with your present life-style, or just someone in search of a healthful and satisfying exercise experience, strength training can play a major part in meeting your needs. All that you need is a willingness and determination to take on a new and exciting challenge.

Misconceptions

Muscle strength training for many years had been associated with physical fitness. The individual who spent hours in the gym lifting weights had always been considered the model of fitness. We know today, however, that strength training, though essential, is only one aspect of total body fitness. In the past many competitive athletes generally avoided strength training because they thought such training exercises were detrimental to the development and maintenance of certain sports skills. Fears that strength training would bring muscle-boundness, loss of flexibility, and reduced coordination were generally accepted. Current research, however, tells us these concepts are erroneous. Strength training is essential for competitive athletes and also plays a role in determining one's physical fitness level. It is not unusual to see weight lifters engaged in long distance running and competitive long distance runners spending more time in weight training. In addition, we now know that resistance training not only leads to increased strength and power but also increases flexibility. The latter benefit puts to rest outdated fears of muscle-boundness.

Muscle Strength, Endurance and Power

The terms strength, muscle endurance and power are sometimes used interchangeably. However, each of these terms has its own definition. Muscle strength is the amount of force that can be exerted by a muscle group for one movement or repetition. Muscle endurance is the ability of the muscle group to maintain a continuous contraction or repetition over a period of time. Power is simply the product of strength and speed and the ability of the muscle to produce high levels of force in a short period of time. The muscle system is the foundation of all physical exercise. No matter what activity you participate in your muscle strength, endurance, and power determine your exercise limits.

In addition, there are other terms that are commonly misused, therefore it seems appropriate to define them before any further discussion.

Weight Lifting is a competitive sport where an individual is judged on the amount of weight that can be lifted relative to weight classification. The clean and press and snatch are the two standardized Olympic events in this competition.

Power Lifting is a competitive sport where the goal is to lift the greatest amount of weight from three exercises (bench press, squat, and dead lift).

Weight Training is an exercise program where free or stationary weights are used for the purposes of increasing strength, endurance, flexibility, skill, and power.

Body Building is an exercise program utilizing free or stationary weights to change body shape and form.

Why Do People Lift?

The reasons people lift weights are as varied and numerous as the people who lift. The weight room may be the most democratic of settings in all of sports and society. People of both sexes, and all ethnic, socio-economic, and age groups lift weight. The reasons may be to improve sport performance, improve physical appearance, improve fitness level, enjoyment of the physical activity or a combination of the preceding.

Benefits of Strength Training

The main areas developed by strength training are muscular strength and endurance, power, flexibility, and body composition. Certain weight training programs can also lead to development in cardiorespiratory endurance. These basic elements of fitness are discussed in detail in chapter 3.

Strength is essential to a variety of everyday physical activities. Even though strength is a relative factor related to the demands of the activity, all individuals need a minimum level of strength. Those with low levels of strength run a greater risk of injury in lifting or engaging in physical activity. Performance in recreational sports and athletics is enhanced by high levels of strength. Strong abdominal muscles provide important protection against lower back problems. Strength training is also an essential part of physical rehabilitation. Common sports injuries such as tennis elbow, rotator cuff, ligament and tendon strains respond well to muscle strength programs. Better posture accompanied by more aesthetic appearance are also benefits from strength training.

Body Building

Many individuals lift weights to improve body shape and form and have little interest in athletic performance. Muscle size and definition take priority over strength and endurance gains. Body building refers to the body's morphology or form and structure that depend mainly on inherited or genetic factors. While your body type or build can be altered only slightly, substantial changes can take place in body composition by decreasing body fat and adding muscle mass. When you exercise you burn more calories than when you are sedentary; therefore you start to lose weight provided your food intake remains the same. A strength and endurance program results in an increase of muscle tissue with a decrease in stored fat. Your body dimensions will change resulting in a slimmer waist, trimmer hips and thighs, and improved overall appearance.

In more detail table 1.1 lists the benefits that you may experience as a result of weight training.

Adaptation

The human body has an amazing capacity to adjust to and benefit from the many physical demands placed upon it. For example, the body is capable of adapting to many kinds of stress and even increasing its efficiency as a result of stressful stimuli. In the case of fitness training, research indicates that repeated physical stress (intensive training) will lead to increases in our functional capacity (strength and endurance). The main purpose in strength training therefore is to stress the body through a variety of exercises so that beneficial adaptations will occur. Strength training is only beneficial as long as it causes the body to adapt to the physical efforts. If the stress is limited, adaptation will not occur. If there is too

Table 1.1   Benefits of Weight Training

Increase in:

Muscle strength
Muscle endurance
Strength of bones and ligaments
Thickness of cartilage
Capillary density in the muscle
Muscle mass (hypertrophy)
Longer duration of effort before exhaustion—stamina
Increased flexibility
Speed and power
Blood volume and hemoglobin
Muscle enzyme levels
Skill
Maximal work capacity
Equalization of muscle development

Decrease in:

Body fat
Stress and tension
Resting heart rate

Additional Benefits May:

Help prevent injuries
Help rehabilitate injuries
Improve function of cardiorespiratory system
Alter metabolism to improve caloric utilization
Recover more quickly from workouts or competitions
Increased self-image and confidence
Improved appearance
Increased feeling of well-being
Naturally induced fatigue and relaxation

much stress, then injury and deterioration will result. An important point to remember is that your physical fitness is largely a reflection of the level of your training. When you work hard, your fitness will be high. However, when you interrupt the intensity of the training, your fitness will decline. Further, individuals with low levels of strength and endurance can look forward to substantial gains in muscular strength and endurance after only a few months of rigorous exercise.

The unique thing about your strength training program is that you are completely in charge. You make all the decisions, set your own goals, and decide when and how to exercise. Your goals in strength training are very clear and measurable with few ambiguities confronting you. Further, you are in a no-lose situation; failure is impossible. There are no records to break, no complex skills to learn; success is there for the asking. There is an immediate payoff; you will be visibly improved by your physical activity. Improved muscle efficiency will produce feelings of increased energy, health, and overall well-being. The benefits of training will be especially noticeable if you are in a poor level of physical condition when you begin your program.

Age and Exercise

Exercise for older persons is a comparatively recent phenomenon brought about by a change in social mores and a new perception of the role of exercise in life. Exercise programs for older persons should consist of flexibility exercises, use of light weights, calisthenics, and continuous fast walking or jogging. Sudden rigorous bursts of exhaustive exercise such as sprinting or lifting very heavy weights should be avoided. Older people should concentrate mainly on endurance activities that are moderate and rhythmic in nature such as jogging, walking, swimming, bicycling, and light weight lifting.

Maximum strength of men and women is generally achieved between the ages of twenty to thirty-five, and significantly high strength levels can be maintained well into advanced age. Normally a progressive decline of muscle strength takes place with age due to a reduced muscle mass brought about primarily by inactivity. Physical training, however, can significantly modify the strength decrement with aging. Older persons can expect improvements when they begin to train in later life no less than younger counterparts.

Finally, if you follow the individualized exercises and guidelines presented in this book, you will be following procedures based upon sound scientific principles, which will benefit your health, and also be a source of continued satisfaction and enjoyment to you.

Glossary

Body Building:
Exercise program, utilizing free and stationary weights, to change body shape and form.

Muscle Endurance:
The ability of a muscle group to maintain a continuous contraction or repetition over a period of time.

Muscle Power:
The product of strength and speed.

Muscle Strength:
The amount of force that can be exerted by a muscle group for one movement or repetition.

Power Lifting:

A competitive event where the goal is to lift the greatest amount of weight for three different exercises [bench press, dead lift and squat]. Explosive power important in this event.

Weight Lifting:

A competitive event where the goal is to lift the greatest amount of weight for two exercises [clean/press and snatch]. Skill, speed and strength are important.

Weight Training:

Exercise program using free or stationary weights for the purpose of increasing strength, endurance, power, skill and flexibility.

Elements of Fitness

2

Objectives

After studying this chapter you should be able to:

1. Describe the importance of strength training.
2. Describe the basic elements of physical fitness.
3. Define muscle strength.
4. Define muscle endurance.
5. Define cardiorespiratory endurance.
6. Define flexibility.

Our misconceptions about fitness are legend. Many people still find it surprising that professional athletes such as baseball players or golfers may have poor cardiorespiratory fitness. Others feel that vibrating and whirlpooling their muscles in a health club will insure fitness, or that by taking a short walk once-a-week fitness will automatically be conferred upon them. Misconceptions stem partly from two varying definitions of fitness, performance related and health related fitness. Performance related fitness refers to many of the tests you may have taken that measure your level of strength, skill, power, endurance, and agility in specific sports. These are performance related tests and measure only limited aspects of fitness. Health related fitness concerns those aspects of our physiological and psychological functioning that afford us some protection against coronary heart disease, problems associated with being overweight, various muscular and skeletal disorders, and the physiological complications of our response to stress. The President's Council on Physical Fitness and Sports defines health related fitness as the ability to carry out daily tasks, with vigor, without undue fatigue, and with ample energy to enjoy leisure-time pursuits and to meet unforeseen injuries. This definition means fitness is a relative term relating to your everyday activities. Some of us need higher levels of fitness than others (physical laborer or competitive athlete). However, all individuals must meet a minimum level of fitness to lead a healthy and productive life.

There are six major elements to physical fitness and the training program you choose should be geared towards the development of these elements. They are muscular strength, muscular endurance, cardiorespiratory endurance, flexibility, and body composition.

Strength (Skeletal-Muscular Strength)

Strength is the ability of a muscle to produce a maximum amount of force. It is measured by the ability to perform one repetition of an exercise at maximum resistance (1 RM). An example of maximum strength would be the greatest amount of weight one can lift in the bench press exercise.

Strength is of major significance in many sports and sport skills. Strength is a significant factor in one's ability to put the shot, throw the javelin, have a high velocity tennis serve, throw a fastball in baseball and softball, and many other sport skills. Strength is also important in sport skills that require a large amount of force be applied to an opponent such as wrestling and football.

Endurance (Skeletal-Muscular Endurance)

Endurance is the ability of a muscle to produce force continually over a period of time. It is measured by the number of repetitions of the movement or skill. If a person can perform thirty-five push-ups, then push-ups are for him or her an endurance skill. If, however, a person can only do one push-up, then for him or her the push-up is a strength skill. The key here is that endurance is the ability to apply force repeatedly or for a prolonged amount of time. Examples of sports requiring endurance are rowing, wrestling, hurdling, sprinting, sprint swimming, and sprint bicycling.

An athlete can continue to produce muscular force for only a short period of time before the energy stored in the muscle is depleted. In movements that require maximum force (strength) this occurs very quickly (one or two repetitions). If less force is required (less than maximal), then the movement can continue for a longer period (endurance).

If the amount of force required of a particular muscle or muscle group is low and the movement is cyclic, allowing a brief rest period (during which another muscle group is producing the movement), then the blood stream can bring nutrients to the muscle cells, and the movement can be prolonged for long periods. Examples of such movement are distance running, swimming, and bicycling. This ability to supply the necessary nutrients to the muscle cells in this fashion is a function of cardiorespiratory endurance.

Cardiorespiratory Endurance

Cardiorespiratory endurance refers to the ability of the respiratory system (lungs and associated blood vessels) and the circulatory system (heart, arteries, capillaries and veins) to supply oxygen and nutrients to the muscle cells so that muscular activity can be continued for prolonged periods of time.

Endurance events such as distance running, cross-country skiing, bicycling, swimming, crew and triathlons are excellent activities for improving cardiorespiratory endurance.

The importance of cardiorespiratory endurance, aside from its role in sport success, is that it can significantly improve your cardiac risk profile.

Aerobic exercises such as running, bicycling, and others are recognized by sport medicine specialists as important in the prevention of heart disease. Heart disease is the number one cause of death in this country, and we should all take steps to improve our risk profile. You should strongly consider including some type of cardiorespiratory endurance exercise into your program. See chapter 12 for more details.

While some sport skills rely more heavily on one aspect of fitness, most athletes need some measure of each of the three components of fitness mentioned (strength, endurance, and cardiorespiratory endurance) as well as flexibility.

Flexibility

Along with strength and endurance, flexibility is an important component of muscular performance. There are two kinds of flexibility, static and dynamic. Dynamic flexibility is defined as the opposition or resistance of a joint to motion. In other words, it is concerned with the forces that oppose movement over any range rather than the range itself. This type of flexibility is difficult to measure and has received little attention in exercise programs and competitive sports.

Static flexibility is defined as the range of motion that can occur at a joint. As a general rule you need enough flexibility to be able to go through the range of motion required for your sport or exercise without any restriction in the movement.

THE FAR SIDE　　By GARY LARSON

The Vikings, of course, knew the importance
of stretching before an attack.

Stretching exercises can increase the range of motion of the joint. Weight lifting, if performed through the full range of motion, can also enhance flexibility. Flexibility exercises are often performed as part of a general warm-up prior to weight lifting. A general warm-up that includes flexibility exercises is recommended, particularly if you are stiff or sore from a previous workout or if the temperature is cold. A stretching program for weight lifting is included in appendix B.

Body Composition

Body composition refers to the proportion of body fat and lean body tissue to total body weight. The relative balance of these components is a better gauge of your fitness level than ordinary body weight. A recommended proportion of body fat for a man in his early twenties is approximately twelve to seventeen percent. For a woman in the same age group, about nineteen to twenty-four percent is recommended. Obesity is one of the most important health problems confronting Americans today. Approximately thirty percent of all men and forty percent of all women weigh fifteen to twenty percent more than they should. Not only will obesity have a negative effect on physical performance, it also has important health ramifications. Being overweight is one of the major risk factors in heart disease. In addition, diabetes and high blood pressure generally accompany obesity. Physical exercise may reduce obesity and directly affect these two common problems. Obesity is also associated with gallbladder disfunction, joint disease, and complications during surgery.

Muscle Power

Power which was discussed in chapter 1 is the ability of the muscles to produce high levels of force in a short time (explosive strength). Power can be increased by strength training and is basic to a number of daily activities and competitive sports. There is also a need for coordination and agility especially if the need for the execution of power is in a particular sports skill such as rebounding in basketball or a lateral movement by a football lineman.

At this point you should think about the requirements of your sport or specific needs and also your strengths and weaknesses in that sport. Most people tend to work on their strengths, as this is easier and more self-satisfying. Working harder on your weaknesses, however, usually produces greater overall improvements.

Chapter 6 contains information to help you determine in which areas you are strong and in which areas of fitness you may require more attention.

Glossary

Aerobic (with Oxygen)
Refers to an activity in which demands of the muscles for oxygen are met by the circulation of oxygen in the blood.

Body Composition
The proportion of body fat to lean body tissue.

Cardiorespiratory Endurance
The ability of the heart to deliver oxygen and nutrients to vital organs of the body.

Flexibility
The extent and range of motion around a joint.

Muscle Endurance
The ability of a muscle to produce force continually over a period of time.

Muscle Power
The ability of the muscle to produce high levels of force in a short time (strength and speed).

Strength
The ability of a muscle to produce a maximum amount of force.

Fundamentals of Weight Training

3

Objectives

After studying this chapter you should be able to:

1. Describe the training goals in strength training.
2. Describe and define the basic principles in a strength training program.
3. Describe the sports training continuum.
4. Describe the process of selecting intensity of training.
5. Define progressive resistance.
6. Define specificity.
7. Define application of force.
8. Describe safety procedures.
9. Define cheating.
10. Define overload.
11. Define repetitions.
12. Define duration.
13. Define frequency.
14. Define intensity.

The muscle system is the foundation of all physical exercise. No matter what activity you participate in, your muscle strength and endurance will significantly affect your exercise limits. It is also important to remember that your muscles are not independent from the rest of the body systems, and conditioning is not limited to the muscles. Your muscles' ability to do work is dependent upon the efficiency of the heart, blood vessels and lungs in providing energy and waste product elimination. Muscles, the heart, blood vessels, and the lungs are simultaneously conditioned because of their interdependence.

More specifically, weight training goals may be directed toward increases in strength and power, increases in muscular endurance or a combination of strength and endurance. Strength and power training is important for power lifters, weight lifters, football linemen, and weight throwers in field events. Muscular endurance training is vital in order to increase the aerobic capacity of the muscles for activities such as cycling, swimming, and rowing. Finally, general conditioning exercises which aim to increase both muscle strength and endurance are vital for success in a number of sports activities. In addition, general conditioning prepares the muscle system to meet everyday demands of individuals not involved in competitive sports. Beyond these three important goals, a large number of individuals participate in weight training programs simply to increase the size and strength of their muscles for personal and aesthetic reasons. Regardless of your goals, a weight training program should incorporate the basic principles outlined in this chapter in order to derive the maximum strength and endurance gains in an efficient and safe manner.

There are certain physiological principles that need to be understood in order to develop a program that will turn your efforts into maximum gains.

Training is stress, and what we try to do while training is to apply stress in the correct amount with the correct frequency to achieve the maximum result. If we apply too much stress or apply the stress too frequently, with insufficient rest, then improvement will not be maximized. Improvement may even be hampered, and detraining (loss of gains) and injury can occur.

Principles

1. All-or-None. When stimulated by the nervous system, a muscle fiber contracts fully, or it does not contract at all. This means that an individual fiber, once stimulated, contracts with all its force. We graduate the amount of force we produce by regulating the number of fibers we innervate or stimulate by the nervous system. To increase strength you try to innervate as many fibers as possible at one time, thus lifting heavy loads with few repetitions. To increase endurance, lighter loads are used and fibers alternate their contractions to allow a rest and recovery period and, thus, a greater number of repetitions.

2. Overload. In order for the muscle to increase its capability, a greater load than normal must be applied. In order for the adaptation to occur, a progressive increase in the amount of work must be performed. For strength increases this is an increase in resistance. For endurance increases this means an increase in repetitions and/or resistance. As an adaption to this increased stress occurs, a greater stress must be imposed for further increases.

3. Specificity of Training. The gains that occur from training will be specific to the type of stress imposed upon the systems. If you do a lot of long-distance running, it improves your cardiorespiratory endurance but does little to improve skeletal-muscular strength. The opposite is also true in that strength training yields little improvement in cardiorespiratory endurance.

4. Use and Disuse. As a muscle is trained, it increases in size and functional ability; it is said to hypertrophy. If training ceases, the muscle begins to detrain, decrease in size, and lose its newly gained capacity; in other words it will atrophy.

5. Individuality. Individuals often respond differently to the same exercise programs. Many factors affect training response including heredity, nutrition, fitness level, motivation, health habits (i.e. rest and sleep), maturity, hormone and enzyme levels, and environmental influences.

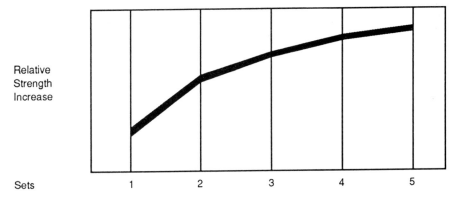

Figure 3.1
Relationship between the number of sets and increases in strength. Reprinted from *Getting Stronger* by Bill Pearl and Gary T. Moran. Copyright © 1986 Shelter Publications, Inc., Bolinas, CA. Reprinted by permission.

Setting Up a Program

After you have given some thought to your goals, the needs of your sport, and evaluated your physical strength and weaknesses, you can refer to figure 3.1 and tables 3.1 and 3.2. They outline the methods and goals of various weight training programs.

Strength Training

The participants of this type of program are competitive weight lifters such as Olympic weight lifters, who perform the clean and press and snatch lifts, and power lifters, who specialize in three lifts: bench press, squat and dead lift. This program is also used by power athletes such as football linemen, shot putters, discus throwers, and others.

These groups of athletes need a large amount of strength to be successful in competition. Their program is designed to increase strength. These athletes lift heavy weights for only a few repetitions, about two to six. When this type of training program is followed, the physiological changes that occur are an increase in the size of the individual muscle fiber and an increase in the ability of the nervous system to stimulate contraction of these fibers. These changes result in an increase in the force produced by the muscle.

Muscular Endurance Training

This program is used by endurance athletes to improve their stamina. The training program is designed to increase the size and number of blood vessels (vascularization) in the muscle and increase the efficiency of the heart and lungs. These changes are a function of increased muscular endurance and are achieved by doing many repetitions, about fifteen to twenty-five with light weights. This pro-

Table 3.1   Sports Training Continuum

	Strength Training	All Around Sports Training	Muscular Endurance Training
Goal	Strength & Power	General conditioning (Strength + endurance)	Muscular endurance (Stamina)
Who Trains This Way	Power lifters Olympic lifters Football linemen Shot putters Etc.	Most athletes General population	Swimmers Rowers Cyclists Distance runners Cross-country skiers Etc.
Physiological Changes	Increase in size of muscle fiber	Some increase in both size of muscle fiber and vascularization	Increase in vascularization, blood supply to muscle
Type of Lifting	Low reps (2–4–6) Heavy weights	Medium reps (8–10–12) Medium weights	High reps (15–25) Light weights

Source: Reprinted from *Getting Stronger* by Bill Pearl and Gary Moran © 1986 Shelter Publications, Inc., Bolinas, California. Reprinted by permission.

cess pumps large amounts of blood into the muscle, and increased muscle size results. The process is known as pumping. Pumping produces significant increases in muscular endurance but only minimal increase in strength.

Body Building

Many successful body builders started out as power lifters or Olympic lifters, acquired significant muscle fiber size, and then switched their program to a body building regime involving pumping action to achieve their massive muscular definition and development. Many body builders will use a strength (power lifting) program during portions of the year and then switch to the endurance (body building) for the competitive portion of the year. This regimen allows them to increase both fiber size and vascularization.

Sport Training

Sport training is the type of weight training that is performed by most competitive athletes. This program is recommended for those individuals interested in maintaining fitness for everyday activities and informal sport and recreation. Table 3.2 summarizes weight training methods with various objectives. (Refer to appendix C for more information on this topic.)

Table 3.2 A summary of the methods of weight training for various objectives (using free weights)

Variable	Power	Strength	Local Muscular Endurance	Size
Sets	4–6	4–6	Maximum	4–6
Repetitions**	3–8	3–8	25–40	Varies*
Method	Explosive, using compensatory acceleration	Moderate cadence	Slow, continuous cadence	Varies*
Rest Intervals	Short pause with relaxation between reps, and 2–6 minutes between sets	Short pause with relaxation between reps, and 2–6 minutes between sets	Allow heart rate to return to manageable level between sets	Varies*

*In size training, variation is the key; for maximal size, use all of the methods listed, interspersing them through each set or between sets. For powerlifters, size resulting from increased contracting elements of a muscle cell (strength system using about 8 reps per set) is most appropriate.
**In deference to the principle of overload, you should always attempt to use the appropriate amount of resistance. The last repetition in each set should be a near-maximal effort. For strength and power training the resistance should exceed 80 percent of your maximum capacity, for muscular endurance above 40 percent, and for size it should vary.
Fredrick Hatfield, Power Lifting, A Scientific Approach. Contempoary Books 1985

Most sports require a combination of strength, muscular endurance, and some measure of cardiorespiratory endurance. Most athletes benefit from a weight training program that yields gains in both strength and muscular endurance. This program is achieved by using a medium amount of resistance and performing a medium number of repetitions, about eight to twelve. The physiological changes that occur with this program are an increase in muscle fiber size and an increase in vascularization.

The sport training program is recommended as an initial or beginning program, even if one's goal is power lifting or body building. Also, if you have never lifted weights or are just returning to lifting, it is recommended that you follow a sport training program, as it will allow you to introduce your skeletal-muscular system and cardiorespiratory system to the rigors of resistance training without the levels of stress that the more specific programs (power lifting and endurance training) would place on you.

Power lifting places enormous stress upon tendons and ligaments as well as the muscle cells. These tissues need time to adjust to these high levels of stress, or injury can occur. Endurance training, because of its high repetitions, produces enormous quantities of biochemical fatigue products from cell metabolism. The buildup of these substances can cause significant muscle soreness, fatigue, and limited mobility. Because it takes time for vascularization to develop, you should work up to endurance training by first following a sport training program. Continue sport training program for eight to ten weeks before shifting toward a strength or endurance program.

Before starting your exercise program you must be aware of three basic principles: intensity, duration, and frequency. Intensity refers to the degree of overload or stressfulness of the exercise, duration is the amount of time utilized for each exercise bout, and frequency is the number of exercises per week. Generally, the more intense, the longer and more frequent the training program, the greater the benefits. Intensity and duration are interrelated, with the total amount of work accomplished being the important factor.

Selecting the Amount of Weight

Generally, to increase muscle strength, the intensity of effort should be near maximum with a low number of repetitions, and to gain muscle endurance, the intensity of effort should be lower with a high number of repetitions. The intensity level for strength gains is believed to be between one and six repetitions maximum. One repetition maximum (1 RM) is the maximum load that you can lift successfully one time through the full range of movement, two repetitions maximum (2 RM) is the amount you can lift successfully two times through the full range of movement, and so on.

Weight training research indicates that weight loads exceeding seventy-five percent of maximum are necessary for promoting strength gains because the most important factor in strength development is intensity. Ten RM weight load usually corresponds to about seventy-five percent of that maximum.

An important factor in beginning your program is selection of the appropriate weight that should be lifted. The key is to select the amount of weight that allows you to perform the right number of repetitions for your program. For example, in the sport training program we recommend that you perform three sets of the following repetitions (10-10-10).

> Set 1—10 repetitions
> Set 2—10 repetitions
> Set 3—10 repetitions

You should choose a weight for set 1 that you can lift ten times (repetitions). You should work hard to perform the tenth repetition. If you could have done more repetitions, then the weight was too light. If you were only able to do six, eight, or nine repetitions, then the weight was too heavy.

The first few weight lifting sessions will be primarily testing sessions to determine the proper weight that you should lift. It is important that you keep accurate records (see record card, appendix G) and have someone spot you during this period.

After your first set of ten repetitions you should rest from one to two minutes before your second set. You may find that on your second set you may be able to perform twelve repetitions of the same weight you used for the first set. If this occurs then you will need to add weight (five to ten lbs.) for the second set to bring your repetitions down to ten. The same may occur with your third set. This increase in strength often occurs and is a result of the influx of blood and increased nerve stimulation to the muscle, making it better able to respond to the demands you make upon it.

To restate our example then, your program might look like this:

Set 1	10 repetitions	X amount of weight
Set 2	10 repetitions	X plus 5 pounds
Set 3	10 repetitions	X plus 10 pounds

Again, please note that the key to the program is the number of repetitions. If, after ten weeks, you want to shade your sport training program towards *strength development,* then you might do 3 sets of 8 repetitions or a program as follows:

Set 1	10 repetitions	X amount of weight
Set 2	8 repetitions	X plus 10 pounds
Set 3	8 repetitions	X plus 15 pounds

If, after ten weeks of a sport conditioning program, you wanted to shade your program towards *endurance development,* you might choose the following type of program:

Set 1	10 repetitions	X amount of weight
Set 2	12 repetitions	X amount of weight
Set 3	12 repetitions	X plus 5 pounds

After you have followed the sport training program for eight to ten weeks, then your skeletal-muscular and cardiorespiratory systems will be in better condition to shift toward a strength or endurance program if you so desire.

Remember! The number of repetitions and the appropriate amount of weight determine whether you are performing a strength, general, or endurance program, not how hard you work. How hard you work will determine your level of success and the amount of gain you achieve. We assume you are willing to work hard, or you would not be reading this book.

Remember the continuum:

Strength Development	2–4–6 repetitions
Sport Training	8–10–12 repetitions
Endurance Development	15–25 repetitions

How Often Should You Lift?

The general rule for weight lifting is to exercise the various muscle groups three times per week. Just as in a running or bicycling program, the best results are achieved when stress is applied in a hard day/easy day fashion. This approach allows for cellular changes to occur at an optimum rate and avoids over-stressing or over-training. In weight training we follow the hard/easy system by working hard one day and then following it with a day off. So a three day a week program would follow a M–W–F or T–Th–Sat routine. This off-day allows the muscles time to recover from the stress that lifting imposes upon them.

Many experienced weight lifters lift more than three times per week (i.e. six days per week), but they will exercise a body part only three times per week. In this program the lifter would work his chest, back and shoulders on M–W–F and his legs and arms on T–Th–Sat. This way each body part is exercised three times per week with a day off in between. This program is called a split-routine and is performed primarily by advanced lifters who perform multiple sets of multiple exercises for a specific body part. Examples of these exercises include regular bench press, inclined bench press, and declined bench press for chest development.

In summary, you should work each body part three times per week. You can do so in a routine in which you do all of your desired exercises three times per week, or a split routine in which you perform a portion of your exercises three times per week and the remaining portion on the alternate days. For the beginning lifter, we recommend exercising three times per week as it is mentally easier to gear yourself up to three workouts per week than six sessions per week.

How Many Sets?

Research in the area of weight training and strength development has found that three to five sets of an exercise produce the most gains. Figure 3.2 demonstrates the effect of various numbers of sets on strength development.

As seen in figure 3.1 you will experience gains with one set and even greater gains with two and three sets. After three sets there is a leveling off of the gains. Performing four or five sets of an exercise produces more gains than three sets, but the amount of this increase is less than occurs during the first three sets. In other words, you have to work harder for fewer results after three sets than you do for the first three sets. The law of diminishing returns prevails. Our recommendation is that you perform three sets of your major exercises. After you are conditioned to the exercises and want greater results, then you can go up to five sets. After five sets the curve flattens out, and little is gained for your efforts.

Overload

Muscle strength only develops when muscles are *overloaded*—forced to contract at maximum or near maximum tension. Muscle contractions at these tension levels produce physiological changes in the muscles, resulting in strength gains. If muscles are not overloaded to this degree, they do not increase in strength or in size (hypertrophy). Muscles adapt only to the load they are subjected to. A maximum overload results in maximum strength gains, whereas a minimum overload produces only minimum strength gains.

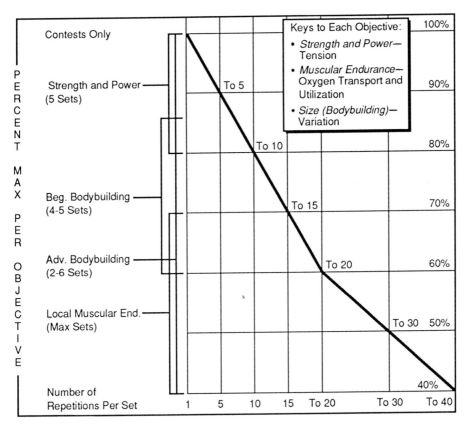

Figure 3.2

Number of repetitions at various intensities. From *Powerlifting: A Scientific Approach* by Frederick C. Hatfield, Ph.D. Copyright © 1985 Contemporary Books, Inc. Reprinted by permission of Contemporary Books, Inc.

Progressive Resistance Exercise

Credit for the development of the first progressive resistance exercise program goes to Milos of Greece, 300 B.C. Milo picked up a calf each day as it grew into a full grown bull. Milo progressivelly lifted a heavier weight each day to overload the muscles and stimulate the muscles to build greater strength. The resistance progressively increased as the calf grew each day and stimulated strength increase. Likewise, the intensity of the load you lift must be progressively increased to ensure future strength gains. If the intensity of the training load is not increased, only existing strength levels are maintained. With progressive overload the muscle responds with an increase in size (hypertrophy) and strength. The same overload response can be used to increase muscular endurance by progressively increasing the number of repetitions performed or the amount of resistance used. If training stops, the lack of stimulus will result in a loss of size (atrophy) and strength.

Specificity

The demands of the exercise must be sufficient to force muscles to adapt, and subsequent muscle adaptations are specific to the type of training performance. This concept is known as *specificity*. For example, aerobic activity develops aerobic capacity, and anaerobic activity develops anaerobic capacity.

Recent research indicates that muscle adaptations are specific to the type of training performed because exercise not only affects muscles but also nerve control of muscles. The nerve pathways appear to become more efficient with continued exercise. The efficiency, however, is specific only to the particular exercise.

Research also indicates that the joint angle of exercise, the type of exercise (that is, isotonic, isometric, or isokinetic), and the speed and range of movement all produce a variety of specific muscle adaptations.

Muscles will adapt specifically to the type of stress that is imposed on them. For example, strength training such as Milo's improves strength while performing many repetitions increases muscular endurance.

It is important that you assess your strengths and weaknesses and the requirements of your sport so that you can train as specifically as possible to maximize your performance increases. (See chapter 6 and appendix C.)

Application of Force

It is also important to maintain a consistent application of force by raising and lowering the weight in a controlled manner. This type of movement subjects the muscles to the same level of stress during both the lifting and lowering phases. Generally the lift phase should take about one to two seconds and the lowering phase approximately two to three seconds. Fast movements require more strength at the beginning of the lift and less force during the later portion of the movement. High speeds of lifting, and lowering are less productive in strength development with the added possibility of causing injury to muscle tissue.

Order of Exercises and Recovery

Progressive training becomes less effective when muscles become fatigued since the training stimulus cannot be maintained at maximum level. Also, overloading a fatigued muscle may lead to soreness and injury. Therefore, follow three simple rules:

1. Exercise large muscle groups before smaller ones. Movements become fatiguing when the small muscles involved in the movement are fatigued. For example, when working the upper body, exercise the chest and back muscles before performing exercises that work primarily the arms or forearm. If not, the fatigued arm muscle may be the limiting factor rather than the chest or back muscles that you are trying to exercise.

2. Arrange your strength exercises so that successive exercises only minimally affect the muscle groups that were just trained previously.
3. Allow forty-eight hours between strength exercises for physiological recovery.

Combination of Exercises and Balance

To promote muscle balance, flexibility and injury free training, opposite muscle groups known as prime movers and antagonists should be exercised. For example, one should complement a quadriceps exercise (leg extension) with hamstring exercises (leg curl). There is a recommended procedure for combining exercises. You should exercise opposite muscle groups such as chest and back during the same workout. This approach ensures balance and harmony of muscle groups that work together in a movement.

A javelin thrower uses his chest and anterior (front) shoulder muscles to throw the javelin and also must use the upper back and posterior (back) shoulder muscles to slow the arm down after the javelin is released. If he develops the chest muscles alone, then he runs the risk of a strength imbalance and injury to back muscles.

The typical combinations of prime movers and antagonists are:

Chest	- Back
Shoulder	- Lats
Biceps	- Triceps
Quadriceps	- Hamstring
Abdominals	- Lower back

Warm-Ups

Warm-ups are necessary to prepare the joint for the activity. Many lifters prepare for the joint movement by performing stretching exercises to move the joint through the range of motion. Often lifters perform a light first set to accomplish this. If you are cold and sore from previous workouts or have been inactive for a while, you should pay particular attention to your warm-up and include jogging and stretching.

Flexibility and Range of Motion

If you exercise through the full range of motion of the joint, you will maintain and likely increase your flexibility. Champion weight lifters and body builders are among the most flexible athletes. The key is to lift through the entire range of motion of each joint. Flexibility exercises are included in chapter 10.

Breathing

It is very important that you breath in a cyclic manner, both inhaling and exhaling with each repetition. Holding your breath throughout the lift can cause oxygen deprivation to the brain and can cause you to pass out. Obviously, this could be dangerous when lifting heavy weights over your head.

When performing a lift, inhale during the easiest part of the lift, *momentarily* hold your breath during the most difficult part, and then exhale when you can comfortably do so. When performing the bench press, for example, inhale as you lower the weight to your chest, momentarily hold your breath while you begin to press the weight upward, and then, during the effort phase of the pressing movement, exhale. As the weights you use become heavier, the momentary period of breath holding may become slightly longer. *You should never,* however, *hold your breath throughout the repetition cycle.* During heavy lifts you need that momentary pause in the breathing cycle (breath holding) to provide a stable support and anchor for the contracting muscles.

If while performing the bench press you exhaled during the beginning of the pressing movement (instead of holding your breath momentarily), the chest would compress during the exhalation at precisely the time you need a stable platform upon which the muscles can perform their contraction and movement.

Positioning

When performing lifts in a standing position (curls, overhead press, etc.) your feet should be a little wider than shoulder width apart, and you should be balanced fore and aft. Many lifters find that wearing shoes or boots with a heel can help offset the shifting of their center of gravity when they lift heavy weights (see fig. 10.8). Lifters sometimes use a board under their heels when performing squats to assist in balance. Hands should be placed approximately shoulder width apart for most lifts, a little wider for the bench press. Thumbs should be wrapped around the bar to insure a stable grip.

Back

In most lifts, such as the dead lift and bent rowing, the back should be kept straight and the lift performed with the legs or arms. This method will help protect the back muscles from strain and injury.

Head

Keep the head and neck straight during almost all lifts. Twisting of the head, neck, and trunk causes injury as the muscles are less efficient when the spine is twisted.

Safety

Safety should concern every athlete in the weight room. To be injured because you or someone else failed to exercise caution and lift safely is truly disheartening. Rules to follow include:

1. Warm up properly.
2. Do not try heavy resistance until you are familiar with the technique you are using.

3. Do not use heavy weights without a spotter (someone to help if you need help).
4. Collars should be used to insure that the weights do not slide off and unbalance the bar.
5. Do not jerk or twist when you lift as these movements significantly increase stress and risk of injury.
6. Use care when performing the following exercises:

a. Full squats—The structure of the knee is such that this exercise can cause ligament and tendon stress in some individuals. Half-squats, to a ninety degree angle between thigh and leg are recommended.

b. Back hyperextensions—Back hyperextensions are a good exercise for strengthening the lower back, however; if too much weight is used too soon, the back muscles can tighten and spasm. Start with light weights and add resistance very gradually.

c. Straight leg sit-ups—Straight leg sit-ups should be avoided as they place significant stress on the lower back. Sit-ups should be done with the knees bent to approximately ninety degrees or more.

d. Dead lift—The dead lift is a good exercise for the thighs and buttocks but you should keep the back straight and lift with the legs. You should keep your head up and eyes on the ceiling; squeeze your buttocks and tighten your abdominals when performing this lift.

Equipment

Many lifters use various accessories to aid their performance and safe lifting. These include:

1. Weight lifting shoes or boots to aid stability.
2. Weight lifting belt to support the lower back.
3. Weight lifting gloves to ensure a good grip and prevent blisters.
4. Weight lifting chalk used on hands ensures a good grip, especially when hands are wet.

Cheating

Cheating is the process of altering a lifting position to enable the lifter to lift more weight or to complete a repetition. An example is arching the back on the bench press. This arching changes the line of pull on the bone and transforms the flat bench press into a form of declined press. This procedure enables the lifter to handle more weight as joint leverage is improved and the lower part of the pectoralis major is used more fully.

Another example is leaning back when doing the biceps curl to complete the exercise. Cheating is an advanced technique; novice lifters should use strict form on their lifts. Even advanced lifters should not cheat on all their sets but merely on the last few sets or last few repetitions of the last set.

Table 3.3   General Principles

1. Warm up prior to lifting weights.
2. Include stretching exercises in your warm-up.
3. Stretching exercises should be done *slowly* through a *full* range of motion.
4. Do not try heavy resistances before you are familiar with the lifting technique you are using.
5. Include all the major muscle groups in your workout.
6. Ensure you involve opposing (prime mover/antagonist) muscle groups and aim for bilateral development.
7. For greater strength development do fewer repetitions (eight or fewer), for a combined strength/muscular endurance response work between eight to twelve reps.
8. Use a technique of lifting and a program workout which suits you personally—as long as it is wisely implemented. Vary the program in such a way so as to maintain interest in what you are doing.
9. Only by keeping accurate records (at least initially) can you effectively gauge your improvements and establish a routine.
10. Some caution might be viewed with relation to:
    a. Performing back hyperextension exercises with weights.
    b. Doing *full* squats.
11. Don't forget:
    a. Your weight training should be supplemented with an aerobic (cardiorespiratory endurance) activity, such as running, bicycling, or swimming.

Advanced lifters use cheating to handle heavier weights than they can normally handle in the strict position. This step can result in their eventually being able to lift that weight with standard form. In short, there is a place for cheating, but it is for advanced lifters and should be used sparingly. Table 3.3 lists a summary of general strength training principles.

Glossary

Atrophy
Decrease in size and functional ability of muscle.

Cheating
The altering of the body's position to change leverage or use more muscle mass to complete a lift.

Duration
The amount of time utilized for each exercise bout.

Frequency
The number of exercises per week.

Hypertrophy
Increase in size and functional capacity of muscle.

Intensity
The degree of overload or stressfulness of the exercise.

Muscle Endurance
The ability of a muscle group to maintain a continuous contraction or repetition over a period of time.

Muscle Strength
The amount of force that can be exerted by a muscle group for one movement or repetition.

One Repetition Maximum
(1 RM) The maximum amount of weight you can successfully lift one time through the full range of motion.

Overload
Forcing a muscle to contract at maximum or near maximum tension.

Progressive Resistance
The progressive increase in load intensity (either weight or repetitions or both).

Specificity
The concept that exercises are specific to the type of training performed.

General Programs

4

Objectives

After studying this chapter you should be able to:

1. Describe a program to develop muscle endurance.
2. Describe a program to develop muscle strength.
3. Describe a program to develop aerobic capacity.

The following programs tables 4.1 through 4.3 have been selected for general conditioning for muscle strength and muscle endurance. You may make minor modifications to these programs depending upon how you respond to the exercise. Time is on your side so don't overstress yourself for the first few weeks. Expect a little muscle stiffness and soreness the first few days. This is your body's way of telling you it has been a long time between workouts. This discomfort should go away in a short time. Tune into your body's signals while you exercise. You know more or less how you feel and how your body responds to exercise. You are the best judge as to what your body is capable of doing.

No single exercise can universally meet the needs of all individuals. However, no matter what exercise program you select it should follow the sequence and fall within the time ranges shown in tables 4.1 through 4.3.

Sport and Fitness Conditioning Programs

The goal of this program is to increase both strength and muscular endurance. This program is appropriate for most athletes and for those beginning a fitness program. The amount of resistance that is utilized will vary from individual to individual, but the principles remain the same. Perform this program three days per week.

You should consider supplementing your sport and fitness conditioning program with an aerobic conditioning program such as running, bicycling, or swimming. Perform the aerobic conditioning program three days per week, on days that alternate with those on which you do the sport and fitness conditioning program. (See chapter 12.)

After you have worked on the conditioning program for eight to ten weeks, you may choose to modify your program toward greater strength or muscular endurance development. The following two programs are designed towards those goals.

Table 4.1 Sport and Fitness Conditioning Program

Weight Training Program (M–W–F)

Exercise	Sets	Repetitions
1. Bench Press	3	10/10/10
2. Seated Rowing	3	10/10/10
3. Bent-Knee Sit-Ups	1	25–75
4. Half Squats	3	10/10/10
5. Triceps Pull-Down	3	10/10/10
6. Seated Dumbbell Curl	3	10/10/10

Table 4.2 Strength Development Program

Weight Training Program A (M–W–F)

Exercise	Sets	Repetitions
1. Bench Press	5	10/8/6/4/2
2. Seated Rowing	5	10/8/6/4/2
3. Military Press	3–5	10/8/6/(4/2)
4. Lat. Pull-Down	3–5	10/8/6/(4/2)
5. Crunch Sit-Ups	3	15–25
6. Trips Pull-overs	3–5	10/8/6/(4/2)
7. Curls	3–5	10/8/6/(4/2)

Weight Training Program B (T–Th–Sat)

Exercise	Sets	Repetitions
1. Squats Half	3–5	10/8/6/(4/2)
2. Sit-ups with Weights	3	10–20
3. Leg Extension	3	10/8/6
4. Leg Flexion	3	10/8/6
5. Back Hyperextension	3	10–20
6. Toe Raises	3	10/8/6

Strength Development Program

The goal of this program is maximum strength development. Perform it six days a week, following weight training program A three days a week, and weight training program B on three alternating days.

You should supplement your weight training program with a cardiorespiratory exercise program of three to five days per week in frequency. Your aerobic program should consist of ten to fifteen minutes of warm-up and flexibility exercises, twenty to forty minutes of aerobic exercise and eight to ten minutes of cool-down. You might consider three days a week of cycling, swimming, or running, as an adjunct to your weight training program. See chapter 12 for a circuit training aerobic program and appendix F for an aerobic running program.

Table 4.3   Muscular Endurance Development Program

Weight Training Program A (M–W–F)

Exercise	Sets	Repetitions
1. a Bench Press	3–5	(18/16) –14–12–10
b Bent Rowing	3–5	(18/16) –14/12/10
2. a Upright Rowing or inclined bench press	3	14/12/10
b Lat. Pull-down	3	14/12/10
3. Alternating Elbow to Knee Sit-Ups	1	50–100
4. a Seated Triceps Dumbbell Curl	3	14/12/10
b Standing Biceps Dumbbell Curl	3	14/12/10

Weight Training Program B (T–Th–Sat)

Exercises	Sets	Repetitions
1. a Leg Press	3	15/12/10
b Back Hyperextension	3	15/15/15
2. a Hip Flexion	3	15/12/10
b Hip Extension	3	15/12/10
3. a Hip Abduction	3	15/12/10
b Hip Adduction	3	15/12/10
4. Bent Knee Sit-Ups	1	50–100
5. a Leg Extension	3	15/12/10
b Leg Flexion	3	15/12/10

Muscular Endurance Development Program

Maximum endurance development (three–six days per week). This program can be done either as a regular routine, three days per week, or as a split routine, six days per week with upper body M–W–F and lower body T–Th–Sat. It is presented here as a split routine.

This program utilizes supersets, a system whereby you alternate exercises, a and b, followed by a rest. You repeat that sequence until the appropriate number of sets are accomplished.

You should supplement your weight training program with a cardiorespiratory endurance program three to seven days per week. You might consider three days a week of cycling and/or three days a week of running as a warm-up to the weight training program.

Motivation and Mental Conditioning

5

Objectives

After studying this chapter you should be able to:

1. Describe the importance of motivation in achieving muscle strength and endurance.
2. Describe guidelines for staying committed.
3. Describe the process of mental preparation in strength training.
4. Define attention, focus, and concentration.

Motivation is the energy and driving force behind what we do in life. Its absence accounts for poor performance, under-utilization of our abilities, and failure to achieve goals. Motivation lies at the heart of our decision to begin a task, to expend effort on the task, and to continue expending effort over a period of time. There is little use in maximized effort, however, unless we know where we are going. Motivation is, therefore, not only the energy that drives our behavior, but it also plays a major role in establishing the goals toward which our energies are directed.

Why We Drop Out

An important question that is often asked is, "Why is it so difficult for many capable individuals to unlearn poor health habits and form new ones?" Is there some undiscovered personality trait that allows some individuals to be able to complete a weight loss program, give up cigarette smoking, and run three miles three times a week? Evidence indicates that two important questions have to be answered before embarking on a program. First, what is the perceived chance of achieving the outcome, and, secondly, what is the value that is placed on the outcome once it has been achieved? Am I capable of achieving increases in strength, and if I do, of what benefit will that increased strength be to me? Regarding the first question, evidence indicates that some individuals are more confident that they will be able to achieve their goals. If you believe you are capable of attaining a goal, you are more likely to achieve it. When faced with obstacles, people who entertain serious doubts about their ability to achieve a goal generally reduce their driving efforts toward their goal or give up altogether. Such factors as past success and encouragement play a vital part of your perception of success.

The more you believe your effort will help you attain your goal, the greater your chance for success. An important point to remember is that the low fit or sedentary individual can look forward to substantial gains in muscular strength and endurance in only a few months of rigorous exercise.

A second consideration is what value we place on the outcomes of our effort. Social science research shows that humans act to maximize gains and minimize losses according to their perceptions of what constitutes a gain or a loss. We will act to ensure benefits to our well-being. We have basic needs that determine why we strive, work, and persevere. These needs must be fulfilled for us to lead a balanced life and to achieve challenging but obtainable goals. We all enjoy the satisfaction of achievement whether it comes from making something with our hands, a promotion at work, or lifting an extra ten pounds. A sense of mastery, a completion of a difficult task, leads to a feeling of self-confidence and well-being. In addition, the physical and psychological benefits outlined in chapter 1 should be important to you.

However, on the other hand be cautious about exercise dependence. For example, some people spend most of their waking hours in the weight room. They clock in more time in their workout shorts than street clothes. They become obsessed and set higher and higher standards, which require more and more of their time, and they lose sight of the important reasons for exercising. Do not strive for unrealistic goals. Place exercise in proper perspective to your personal goals in life. The purpose for most individuals is to improve themselves and to achieve a realistic self-concept.

A Few Tips for Staying Committed

1. Make a list of the physiological and psychological benefits you expect to achieve from your program.
2. Think about past successes in your life, how you achieved them, why they were important to you, and their significance in the long and short term.
3. Evaluate your chances of success by evaluating your present status, your capabilities, and your limitations. Don't underestimate your potential. Remember! No one fails when he or she exercises.
4. Think how a training program will benefit you. Are you convinced that the physical and psychological changes that result from exercise will be beneficial?
5. Set both short and long term goals. Be honest with yourself about what you can accomplish. Set realistic and achievable goals.
6. Plan a strategy by making a list of what you need to do. This book will help you in this area.
7. Find a support group; you might find it beneficial to exercise with one or more friends. A group can provide feedback and personal support.
8. Vary your exercises to avoid boredom. Introduce variation, be creative, select exercises that bring out new skills, and extend and challenge old ones. Music also helps.

9. Stay within your limits and don't be obsessive about exercising. Don't worry about missing a few exercise periods. Don't be awed by others with more strength. Individualize your program. Don't compete with others.
10. Record your progress. *Keep records but don't keep score.*
11. Be patient. Nothing worthwhile happens overnight. There will be slumps and bad days and temporary loss in skill. Don't expect instant success. Change will occur.

Why Do People Lift?

The reasons that people lift weights are as varied and numerous as the people who lift. The weight room may be the most democratic of settings in all of sports and society. People of both sexes and all ethnic, socio-economic, and age groups lift weights. The reasons they lift may include; to improve sport performance, improve physical appearance, improve fitness level, enjoy a physical activity, or a combination of some or all of the above.

Regardless of the reason or reasons, almost everyone who lifts weights experiences an improved self-image. Strength truly builds confidence. An increase in self-confidence can go a long way in improving one's sport performance, physical appearance, and out look on life.

Mental Preparation

Today's athlete can find no more fertile area in which to improve his or her performance than that of psychological preparation. The importance of this avenue for improving both training and contest performance has been known for years. The Soviet and East German national teams have had a sport psychologist assigned to each team for twenty years. In the United States many professional and university teams use sport psychologists to help improve individual and team performance. In addition, many individual athletes not associated with teams are using sport psychology techniques and exercises to improve their training and performance.

We will concentrate primarily on the psychological techniques that are most pertinent to improve weight training performance, but we urge you to look further into additional techniques and exercises that may be pertinent to your particular sport or activity. A recommended reading list follows this chapter.

In weight training the majority of our efforts go towards training. Thus, if we can use some psychological techniques successfully, we can improve our training efforts, and gains will be greater.

Attention, Focus, and Concentration

The terms attention, focus, or concentration refer to the ability to direct our thoughts and efforts to a specific task and ignore extraneous stimuli. In weight training, you must be able to focus your attention on the lift in order to achieve maximum performance. This process is enhanced by limiting external stimuli that divert your attention and by narrowing your attention to the lift.

Visualization and Imagery

One technique that can be useful in focusing your attention is visualization. It is commonly used by many athletes today. The process involves rehearsing the lift in your mind and seeing (visualizing) yourself performing the lift. You imagine through mental rehearsal the process of lowering the weight, the feeling of its weight, the power with which you stop the weight and change its direction upward, and the force of exertion as you press it upward. In your mind's eye you watch yourself doing this as you feel the sensation of doing so. You are rehearsing a successful lift. This is a particularly good technique to use when you are trying for a maximum lift.

Positive Self-Thoughts

One of the obstacles to better performance for almost every athlete is the recurrent appearance of negative thoughts. Negative thoughts occur because of the influence of past experiences, listening to the negative thoughts of others, or listening to our own self-doubts. The results of these inputs are that we often focus on a negative outcome rather than a positive outcome.

We often fail to lift a certain weight because we have convinced ourselves that we cannot do so. The way to deal with negative thoughts or self-doubts is to immediately change those thoughts to positive ones so that you are rehearsing success rather than failure.

The following are examples of changing negative thought to positive ones.

Negative Thoughts	Change to Positive Thoughts
I can't . . .	I can do it. I have done it many times before.
I won't be at my best because . . .	I have done everything I can do to prepare.
The heat is so bad I cannot do anything . . .	The heat creates a greater challenge.
I am really nervous and anxious . . .	The last time I felt this way, and I performed my best.
I am afraid that I will make a fool of myself . . .	Unless I face the challenge and take the risk, I'll never know what I can accomplish.
I don't want to fail . . .	What is absolutely the worst thing that could happen to me? I could lose. If so, I will work harder to try to prevent that.
What is the worst thing that could happen?	I will be disappointed if things do not turn out as I want them to; however, I'll work harder to ensure success.
You stupid jerk . . .	Why don't you try to do _____ next time? It might be a better approach than the one you are using now.
I don't think I am prepared . . .	I have practiced and trained hard for this performance so I am prepared to do well.
I am tired, I can't go on . . .	It is almost over, I know I can finish. The difficult part has passed.
I am getting worse instead of better . . .	I need to set daily goals and evaluate my progress on a regular basis.
I have failed to get beyond this point every time I have faced it . . .	I can learn from my mistakes. This time I will do what I need to do to be successful.
I don't care whether I win or lose . . .	I have put too much time and effort into preparing for this event not to put forth everything I can to be successful.
I lost again. I'll never be a winner . . .	I can learn from losing. I need to talk with a coach to get some help regarding those things I need to improve.
I will never be as good as . . .	With more work, I can improve my skills and my performance.
It is not fair. I work just as _____ but I don't do as well . . .	I may have to work harder than some to accomplish the same level. I am willing to work as hard as I have to because I want to succeed.
I never seem to be able to do this . . .	This time I am going to think through and mentally prepare so that I can do it . . .

Adapted from "The Athletes Guide to Sports Psychology", by Harris & Harris.

There are many other aspects to sport psychology; the preceding was a brief introduction to the area. If you would like more information, we suggest the following books:

1. The Athletes Guide to Sports Psychology: Mental Skills for Physical People. Harris & Harris, 1984 Leisure Press, N.Y.
2. Sports Psyching, Playing Your Best Game All of the Time. Tatko & Tosi, 1976, J. P. Tharcher Inc., Los Angeles.
3. Peak Performance, Mental Training Techniques of the World's Greatest Athletes. Garfield and Bennett, 1984, J. P. Tharcher Inc., Los Angeles.

Glossary

Attention/Focus/Concentration
The ability to direct our thoughts and effort to a specific task and ignore extraneous stimuli.

Imagery
The mental picture we focus upon during visualization, such as the successful completion of a lift. These images help us in the process of performing our intended tasks.

Motivation
The basic reason why we strive, work, and persevere toward our goals.

Visualization
The process of forming a mental picture of an act that we will perform. Visualization can also be described as the act of rehearsing the successful completion of an act that we wish to perform.

Evaluation and Self-Assessment

6

Objectives

After studying this chapter you should be able to:

1. Describe the importance of fitness evaluation.
2. Define muscle strength and endurance.
3. Define cardiovascular endurance.
4. Define body density.
5. Define flexibility.
6. Explain tests for muscle strength and endurance.
7. Explain tests for cardiovascular endurance.
8. Explain tests for body density.
9. Explain tests for flexibility.

It is essential that you make an objective evaluation of your present muscle strength and endurance in order to determine the focus of your training program. Muscle endurance is to some degree dependent upon muscle strength. However, it is possible to have a high level of muscle strength and a low level of muscle endurance. Also, this evaluation will enable you to set reasonable strength training goals and prevent unnecessary stress on your body's systems.

Also included in a complete physical fitness evaluation are tests of cardio-respiratory endurance, body composition and flexibility.

Because of the many variables found in fitness tests, such as sex, age, height, flexibility and motivation, these tests are not precise measures and are subject to error. They should be used only as general guidelines for outlining your fitness program and as indicators of how you compare with others of your age and sex.

Muscle Strength Test

Muscle strength can be easily assessed by the one-repetition maximum test (1 RM), the maximum amount of weight you can successfully lift once. Four tests are utilized; bench press (fig. 10.1), leg press (fig. 10.25), biceps curl (fig. 10.11), and shoulder press (fig. 10.8). For each, determine the greatest weight that you can lift just once for that particular lift. Begin with a weight that you can lift comfortably. Then keep adding weight until you can lift the weight correctly just one time. If you can lift the weight more than once, more pounds should be added until the true 1 RM is reached.

Table 6.1   Muscle Strength Tests

Male	Percentage of Weight Lifted	Very Poor	Poor	Average	Good	Very Good	Excellent	Superior
				Fitness Level				
Bench press	_____	50	75	100	110	120	140	150
Leg press	_____	160	180	200	210	220	230	240
Biceps curl	_____	30	40	50	55	60	70	80
Shoulder press	_____	40	50	67	70	80	110	120

Female	Percentage of Weight Lifted	Very Poor	Poor	Average	Good	Very Good	Excellent	Superior
				Fitness Level				
Bench press	_____	40	60	70	75	80	90	100
Leg press	_____	100	120	140	145	150	175	190
Biceps curl	_____	15	20	35	40	45	55	60
Shoulder press	_____	20	30	47	55	60	60	80

Source: From *Health and Fitness through Physical Activity* by M. L. Pollock, J. H. Wilmore, and S. M. Fox. Copyright © 1978 by John Wiley & Sons. Reprinted with permission of the publisher.

For each muscle group, divide the total amount of weight lifted by your present body weight in pounds to determine the percentage of weight lifted. Now find your percentages in table 6.1. This table is based upon the percentage of your body weight you can lift for each of the exercises.

(A more comprehensive muscle strength list may be found in appendix D.)

Muscular Endurance

Table 6.2 can be used to assess your muscular endurance.

The norms are based on a college age population. (See chapter 10 for proper exercise positions.)

Precaution Regarding the One RM Maximum Strength Test

Older individuals, those who have been sedentary for some time, and those with a low level of strength should not attempt the 1 RM test for maximum strength until approximately week eight of their training program. After eight weeks they will have developed sufficient skill, flexibility, and familiarization with lifting so that there is little chance of possible injury with the 1 RM test. The 10 RM level (see chapter 3) should be used in training up until the eighth week. Your 10 RM at a particular weight is equal to approximately seventy-five percent of your 1

Table 6.2 Dynamic Muscular Endurance Test Battery

	Percent of Body Weight Lifted		
Exercise	Men	Women	Repetitions (max = 15)
Arm curl	0.33	0.25	_____
Bench press	0.66	0.50	_____
Lateral pull-down	0.66	0.50	_____
Triceps extension	0.33	0.33	_____
Leg extension	0.50	0.50	_____
Leg curl	0.33	0.33	_____
Bent-knee sit-up			_____
		Total repetitions (max = 105) =	_____

Total Repetitions	Fitness Category*
91–105	Excellent
77–90	Very good
63–76	Good
49–62	Fair
35–48	Poor
<35	Very poor

Source: Heyward, V. *Design for Fitness*. Minneapolis: Burgess, 1984, p. 47. Used by permission.
*Based on data for 250 college-age men and women.

RM. This can be used to estimate an individual's 1 RM in situations when a 1 RM attempt is inappropriate. Physically active college students may be given the 1 RM test during the second or third week. However, the test for muscular endurance can be safely administered during the first weeks of the training program.

Push-Ups

Start in a standard "up" position for a full push-up, with your weight on your toes and hands. (If you have limited upper body strength, you can perform this test with your knees bent and your weight on your knees and hands.) Figure 6.1 illustrates both positions. Your partner should place his or her fist on the floor beneath your chest. Lower yourself until your chest touches your partner's fist. Keep your back straight while raising to an "up" position. Count the number of consecutively performed push-ups and then refer to table 6.3 to determine your fitness level.

Figure 6.1
Push-Ups.

Bent-Knee Sit-Ups

Even though it is difficult to measure abdominal muscle endurance, the bent-knee sit-up is the best test available. The sit-up, when performed with the knees bent, depends not only on the abdominal muscles but also the hip flexors.

Lie on your back. Cross your arms on your chest and place your hands on opposite shoulder. Your knees should be bent at about ninety degrees with both feet flat on floor and no more than eighteen inches in front of the buttocks. Your partner should hold your feet stationary by grasping them at the ankles. Complete as many sit-ups as possible in one minute. Warm up with a few sit-ups before the test.

Refer to table 6.4 to determine your fitness level.

Table 6.3 Push-Up Test

Standard Push-Up (weight on toes)

Age (years)	Fitness Level						
	Superior	Excellent	Very Good	Good	Average	Poor	Very Poor
15–29	Above 51	51–54	45–50	35–44	25–34	20–25	15–19
30–39	Above 41	41–44	35–40	25–34	20–24	15–20	8–14
40–49	Above 36	35–39	30–35	20–29	14–19	12–14	5–11
50–59	Above 31	31–34	25–30	15–24	12–14	8–12	3–7
60–69	Above 26	26–29	20–25	10–19	8–9	5–7	0–4

Modified Push-Up (weight on hands and knees)

Age (years)	Fitness Level						
	Superior	Excellent	Very Good	Good	Average	Poor	Very Poor
15–29	Above 48	46–48	34–45	17–33	10–16	6–9	0–5
30–39	Above 38	33–37	25–33	12–24	8–11	4–7	0–3
40–49	Above 33	29–32	20–28	8–19	6–7	3–5	0–2
50–59	Above 26	21–25	15–21	6–14	4–5	2–3	0–1
60–69	Above 20	15–19	5–15	3–4	2–3	1–2	0–

Source: From *Health and Fitness through Physical Activity* by M. L. Pollock, J. H. Wilmore, and S. M. Fox. Copyright © 1978 by John Wiley & Sons. Reprinted with permission of the publisher.

Table 6.4 Bent Knee Sit-Ups Endurance Test

Age (years)	Fitness Level						
	Very Poor	Poor	Average	Good	Very Good	Excellent	Superior
Males							
17–29	0–17	17–35	36–41	42–47	48–50	51–55	55+
30–39*	0–13	13–26	27–32	33–38	39–43	44–48	48+
40–49	0–11	11–22	23–27	28–33	34–38	39–43	43+
50–59	0–8	8–16	17–21	22–28	29–33	34–38	38+
60–69	0–6	6–12	13–17	18–24	25–30	31–35	35+
Females							
17–29	0–14	14–28	29–32	33–35	36–42	43–47	47+
30–39*	0–11	11–22	23–28	29–34	35–40	41–45	45+
40–49	0–9	9–18	19–23	24–30	31–34	35–40	40+
50–59	0–6	6–12	13–17	18–24	25–30	31–35	35+
60–69	0–5	5–10	11–14	15–20	21–25	26–30	30+

Source: Reprinted by permission of the American Alliance for Health, Physical Education, Recreation, and Dance, 1900 Association Drive, Reston, Virginia 22091.
*The value of ages over thirty is estimated.

Figure 6.2
Sit and reach test.

Table 6.5 Sit and Reach Test

Sit and Reach Score	Fitness Level	Sit and Reach Flexibility Level
11 in or less	Very poor	_____
12 to 13 in	Poor	_____
14 to 16 in	Average	_____
16 to 18 in	Good	_____
20 to 21 in	Very good	_____
22 to 23 in	Excellent	_____
24+ in	Superior	_____

Source: Standards for Sit and Reach and Back Hyperextension, "Health Improvement Program," National Athletic Health Institute.

Test for Flexibility

The sit and reach test is a measure of trunk and hamstring *flexibility* (the range of motion about a joint). (Individuals with poor flexibility should stretch before attempting this test.)

Sit and Reach Test

Sit with your legs extended directly in front of you and with the backs of your knees pressed against the floor. Do not hyperextend knees or lock them in position. Your feet should be placed up against a stool to which a yardstick has been attached. The yardstick should be on top of the stool, with the fourteen-inch mark placed at the point where your foot contacts the stool. Place the index fingers of both of your hands together and reach forward as far as possible, keeping your knees in contact with the floor at all times (fig. 6.2). From the yardstick, note the distance you are able to reach. Find your score in table 6.5 to determine your sit and reach flexibility level.

Determine Your Cardiorespiratory Endurance Level

The chief means of evaluating cardiorespiratory efficiency is to determine the body's capacity to consume oxygen at a maximum rate. The assessment of oxygen uptake through laboratory testing is the most accurate method but requires a good deal of time and sophisticated equipment and is impractical for self-testing. The one and a half mile run test can be used to measure the amount of maximum oxygen uptake by determining the heart rate response to the exercise.

1.5 Mile Run

The 1.5 mile test can be run on an oval track or on a straightaway. You should only perform this test if you have been training to run this distance and are in good physical condition. If you are over thirty-five years of age, you should not take this test unless you have had a normal stress electrocardiogram. If you become overtired while running, slow down to a jog or walk. Do not unduly overstress yourself. Keep track of the amount of time it takes you to run 1.5 miles, and then find your fitness level in table 6.6.

Test for Body Composition

Body composition refers to the proportion of lean body tissue to total body weight. The recommended percentage of body fat for adult males is twelve to seventeen percent, for adult females nineteen to twenty-four percent.

The skin fold test for determination of body fat is based on the relationship of subcutaneous fat (fat just below the skin) to total lean body tissue. The method is subject to errors of as much as three to fifteen percent, plus or minus the actual body fat percentage.

To perform the test you need a pair of skin calipers. Hold the skin fold between the thumb and index finger. Release the tension on the calipers slowly so that they pinch the skin fold as close as possible to your fingers. Three measures are required for both male and female. The chest, thigh and abdomen for the male and the triceps, thigh and iliac crest for the female. See figures 6.3 through 6.7.

After taking the three skin fold measurements appropriate to your sex, total the measurements on the nomogram in figure 6.8. Use the straight edge to connect the point on the left that corresponds to your age with the point on the far right that corresponds to the sum of your three skin fold measurements. Then read the percentage of body fat from the center male or female scale.

Table 6.6 Aerobic Fitness Guidelines for the 1.5 Mile Test (Times in Minutes)

Fitness Category		Age (years)	
		13–19	*20–29*
I. Very poor	(men)	>15:31*	>16:01
	(women)	>18:31	>19:01
II. Poor	(men)	12:11–15:30	14:01–16:00
	(women)	16:55–18:30	18:31–19:00
III. Fair	(men)	10:49–12:10	12:01–14:00
	(women)	14:31–16:54	15:55–18:30
IV. Good	(men)	9:41–10:48	10:46–12:00
	(women)	12:30–14:30	13:31–15:54
V. Excellent	(men)	8:37–9:40	9:45–10:45
	(women)	11:50–12:29	12:30–13:30
VI. Superior	(men)	<8:37	<9:45
	(women)	<11:50	<12:30

*< Means "less than"; > means "more than."
From THE AEROBICS PROGRAM FOR TOTAL WELL-BEING by Dr. Kenneth H. Cooper. Copyright © 1982 by Kenneth H. Cooper. Reprinted by permission of the publisher, M. Evans and Company, Inc., New York, New York 10017.

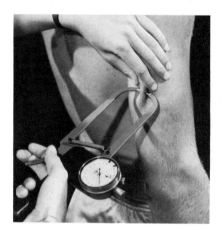

Figure 6.3
Triceps skinfold measurement. Locate a vertical skinfold on the back of the arm halfway between the tip of the acromion process (bony projection on the tip of the shoulder) and the olecranon process (rear point of the elbow), with the arm hanging in a relaxed position.

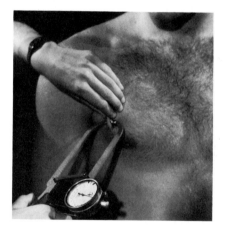

Figure 6.4
Chest skinfold measurement. Locate a point over the outside edge of the pectoralis major muscle just adjacent and medial to the armpit. The skinfold should run diagonally between the shoulder and the opposite hip.

Age (years)			
30–39	*40–49*	*50–59*	*60+*
>16:31	>17:31	>19:01	>20:01
>19:31	>20:01	>20:31	>21:01
14:44–16:30	15:36–17:30	17:01–19:00	19:01–20:00
19:01–19:30	19:31–20:00	20:01–20:30	21:00–21:31
12:31–14:45	13:01–15:35	14:31–17:00	16:16–19:00
16:31–19:00	17:31–19:30	19:01–20:00	19:31–20:30
11:01–12:30	11:31–13:00	12:31–14:30	14:00–16:15
14:31–16:30	15:56–17:30	16:31–19:00	17:31–19:30
10:00–11:00	10:30–11:30	11:00–12:30	11:15–13:59
13:00–14:30	13:45–15:55	14:30–16:30	16:30–17:30
<10:00	<10:30	<11:00	<11:15
<13:00	<13:45	<14:30	<16:30

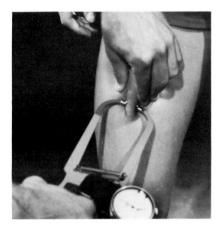

Figure 6.5
Thigh skinfold measurement. Locate a
vertical skinfold in the anterior midline of the
thigh, halfway between the hip and the knee
joint. Place your body weight on the
opposite leg while taking the measurement.

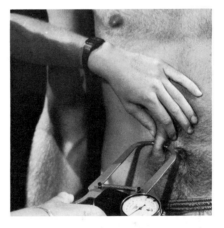

Figure 6.6
Abdomen skinfold measurement. Locate a
vertical skinfold adjacent to the umbilicus.

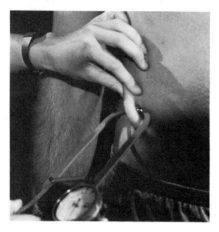

Figure 6.7
Iliac crest skinfold measurement. Locate a
vertical skinfold over the iliac crest (point of
the hip) in the midaxillary line (middle of the
armpit).

Glossary

Body Composition
The proportion of body fat to lean body tissue.

Cardiorespiratory Efficiency
The ability of the heart to deliver oxygen to all of the organs of the body.

Flexibility
The extent and range of motion about a joint.

Muscle Endurance
The ability of a muscle to produce force continually over a period of time.

Skinfold Test
The method of estimating body fat by measuring subcutaneous fat with
skinfold calipers.

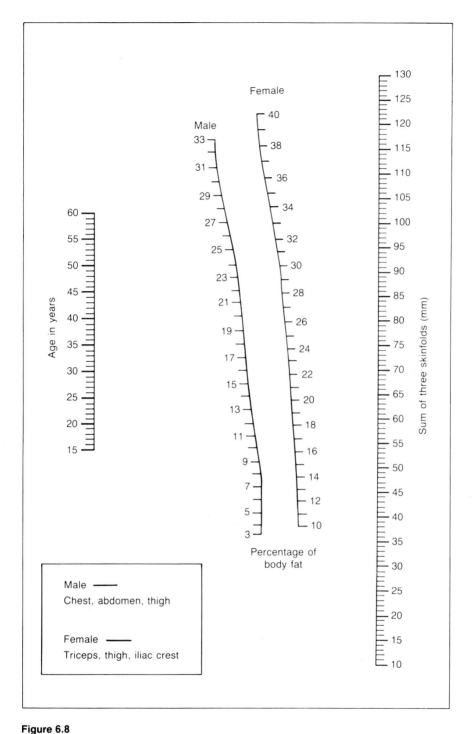

Figure 6.8

Nomogram for the determination of percentage of body fat for the sum of the chest, abdomen, and thigh skinfolds of males fifteen years of age and above, and for the sum of the triceps, thigh, and iliac crest skinfolds of females fifteen years of age and above. (See next page.) Adapted from W. B. Baun, M. R. Baun, and P. B. Raven, "A Nomogram for the Estimate of Percent Body Fat from Generalized Equations," *Research Quarterly for Exercise and Sport* 52(1981): 380–84. Reprinted by permission of the American Alliance for Health, Physical Education, Recreation and Dance, 1900 Association Drive, Reston, Virginia 22091.

Muscles

7

Objectives

After studying this chapter you should be able to:

1. Describe the structure of a skeletal muscle.
2. Describe the physiology of a muscle contraction.
3. Define hypertrophy and atrophy.
4. Describe muscle soreness.

The basic function of skeletal muscles is to contract. This contraction enables human movement to occur. Over 600 skeletal muscles provide us with the capability to perform all manner of voluntary movement. Each voluntary muscle is a separate structure in its own right, containing connective tissue, nerves, and blood vessels. The muscles comprise approximately forty-two percent of the body weight in men and thirty-six percent in women.

Structure of Skeletal Muscle

If you were to closely examine a skeletal muscle, you would find that each muscle has its own outer covering of connective tissue called epimysium. As seen in figure 7.1, the extension of the outer connective tissue at the end of the muscle forms the tendon, which connects and anchors the muscle to the bone. If the epimysium is peeled away from the body of the muscle, a number of bundles called fasciculi are revealed. Each bundle is surrounded by its own connective tissue structure called perimysium. Contained within this muscle bundle are the individual muscle fibers. Each fiber (some the size of a human hair) is surrounded by a covering of connective tissue called endomysium.

Each muscle fiber is composed of hundreds of cylindrical shaped structures called myofibrils. A sheath or membrane covers each fiber, separating it from the surrounding fluid. The myofibrils contain the tiny protein filaments whose actions are responsible for the contraction of the myofibrils and, in turn, the muscle. The myofibrils are immersed in the fluid portion of the fiber called sarcoplasm. The sarcoplasm contains enzymes to power the mitochondria, which are the power packs of the cell. Myofibrils contain two kinds of protein filaments, thick ones composed of the protein myosin and thin ones composed of the protein actin.

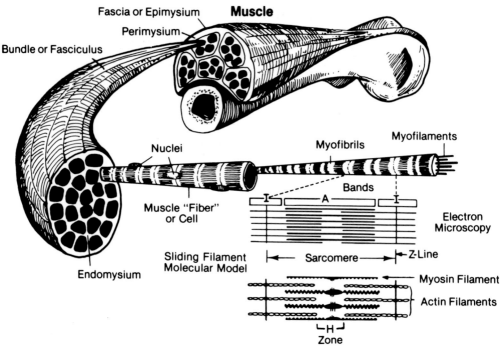

Figure 7.1

Structural design of human skeletal muscle. From Jack H. Wilmore and David L. Costill, *Training for Sport and Activity,* 3rd ed. Copyright © 1988 Wm. C. Brown Publishers, Dubuque, Iowa. All Rights Reserved. Reprinted by permission.

These proteins are geometrically aligned throughout the muscle. As seen in figure 7.2, the smallest unit of the myofibril is the sarcomere, which is the distance between two Z-lines. When the muscle is stimulated by the nervous system, this small unit will contract. The A-band, the dark portion of the sarcomere, consists of both actin and myosin filaments with the actin filaments attached to the Z-lines. The tiny projections extending from the myosin filaments or the actin filaments are called the myosin cross bridges (fig. 7.3). These tiny cross bridges are instrumental in the shortening of the muscle. When the muscle contracts, the actin filament slides over the myosin filament toward the center of the sarcomere in a coupling process where the myosin cross bridges form a temporary bond with the actin filaments. This coupling process is dependent on the release of calcium ions stored in a membranous structure called the sarcoplasmic reticulum (see fig. 8.1). Active sites on the actin filaments are covered by troponen and tropomyosin proteins. When the calcium ions are released they bind with troponen and cause a change in tropomyosin so that it exposes active sites on the actin filament. When coupling takes place, the cross bridges swivel in a manner that causes the actin filaments to slide over the myosin filaments. This process activates the enzyme ATPase (adenosine triphosphatase) that breaks down ATP (adenosine triphosphate) stored on the crossbridges. ATP provides energy for the action between

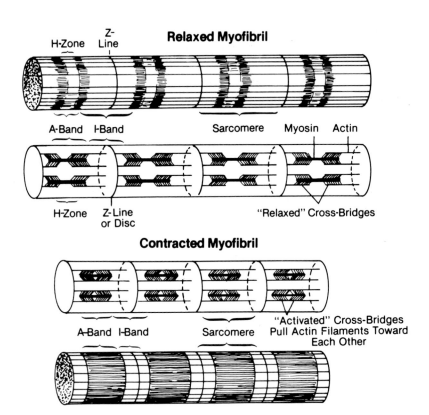

Figure 7.2
The sequence of events that takes place within a myofibril during contraction. From Jack H. Wilmore and David L. Costill, *Training for Sport and Activity*, 3d ed. Copyright © 1988 Wm. C. Brown Publishers, Dubuque, Iowa. All Rights Reserved. Reprinted by permission.

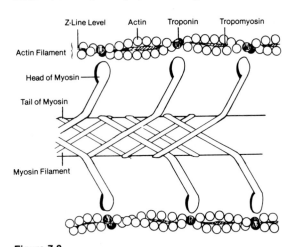

Figure 7.3
Myosin molecules have projections that extend toward nearby actin filaments. From Jack H. Wilmore and David L. Costill, *Training for Sport and Activity*, 3d ed. Copyright © 1988 Wm. C. Brown Publishers, Dubuque, Iowa. All Rights Reserved. Reprinted by permission.

actin and myosin. For more shortening to occur, the cross bridges must break bonds already formed and bind to other active sites reloaded with ATP on the actin filament. This process is called recharging. When neural stimulation stops, calcium ions are pumped back into the sarcoplasmic reticulum, the cross bridges uncouple, and the muscle relaxes.

Agonist and Antagonist

Muscles and muscle groups work in harmony to produce a movement. When the leg is extended, the muscle responsible for that movement is called the agonist or prime mover. Another muscle, the antagonist, has to relax to allow for smooth movement. In leg extension movements, the quadriceps are the agonists, and the hamstrings are the antagonists. The antagonists are also capable of resisting agonist action and are responsible for movement in the opposite direction. The antagonists of the prime mover that extends the leg are responsible for flexing it. If both agonists and antagonists contract at the same time, the part they act upon will remain stationary. Smooth coordinated movements depend upon the prime mover and antagonist working in harmony. It is therefore important to strengthen both groups of muscles and not one at the expense of the other.

Tendons

Tendons are the extension of the outer cover of the muscle and anchor the muscle to the bone. They have the appearance of white glistening cords or bands.

Ligaments

Ligaments are strong flexible bands or capsules of fibrous tissue that help hold the bones together at the joints. They play a significant role in determining the range of motion of the joint.

Atrophy

With a lack of neural stimulation and exercise, a wasting process may take place in which the muscle becomes smaller and weaker. This process, called atrophy, is often apparent when a limb has been in a cast or immobilized for an extended period of time.

Slow and Fast Twitch

Human muscles contain three types of muscle fibers: a slow-twitch Type I *red fiber* and two types of fast-twitch Type II *white fibers*. Each fiber type is structurally and chemically equipped to perform work for long or short periods of time. For example, fast-twitch fibers are preferentially used for short-term, high intensity exercises such as sprinting, while slow-twitch fibers are used during longer, less intensive exercise such as long-distance running.

Exercise cannot change the types or numbers of fibers in your muscles, as these characteristics (or traits) are inherited. However, the efficiency of both red and white muscle fibers can be increased through proper training methods. A specific type of exercise must be used to improve the efficiency of a given fiber type. For example, to increase the metabolic potential of fast-twitch fibers, high intensity exercise of few repetitions must be used. Conversely, exercises of longer duration with lower intensities increase the metabolic potential of slow-twitch fibers.

Fast-twitch fibers produce greater force than slow-twitch fibers. As a result individuals with a greater cross sectional area of fast-twitch fibers are capable of generating greater strength. Fast-twitch units, however, are quick to fatigue from very intense contractions which demand high rates of force development.

Hypertrophy

Hypertrophy is an increase in the size and functional capacity of a muscle. There are two types of hypertrophy, transient and chronic. Transient hypertrophy is caused by the pumping action of the muscle and results in fluid accumulation in the muscle. This temporary enlargement disappears shortly after termination of exercise. In chronic (or true) hypertrophy the muscle growth results from enlargement of the muscle fiber. This growth is directly related to the increased synthesis of protein that increases the thickness of the myofibrils. Tension overload may also stimulate proliferation of connective tissue, capillarization, and satellite cells that surround the muscle fibers and improve the *structural integrity of ligaments and tendons*. The greatest hypertrophy is seen in those muscles that in everyday activity do the least work in relation to their genetic potential. The tension a muscle develops during exercise is a stimulus for increased uptake of amino acids and enhanced synthesis of protein. In addition, it is thought that a breakdown and buildup process takes place. This theory holds that intensive training breaks down muscle protein that then rebuilds between training sessions and leads to a super compensation and an increase in muscle size. However, the exact cellular mechanism by which resistance training results in increased muscle size is still unknown.

The degree of hypertrophy will depend not only on the severity of the overload but the total duration of the overload. However, one must be cautioned about individual exceptions to this principle. For instance, individuals with a large

number of fibers may have an advantage in terms of their capacity for training over those with fewer fibers, particularly in body building. Also, evidence indicates that body builders who engage in high volume, low intensity training gain increased size of slow-twitch fibers and increased capillarization. Power lifters who engage in low volume, high intensity training gain increased size of fast-twitch fibers with decreased capillarization.

Hyperplasia

Hyperplasia is an increase in the number of muscle fibers. Considerable controversy still exists regarding whether or not heavy resistance training results in an increase in muscle fibers (hyperplasia). Recent research has criticized the methodology used in former studies that found some evidence of fiber splitting. The differences in research results may also be due to differences in the mode of training as well as methodology. The consensus is that weight training or other exercises do not result in an increase in the number of muscle fibers, rather they increase the size and functional capacity of existing fibers.

Muscle Soreness

Many individuals engaged in rigorous exercise encounter muscle soreness. Two different patterns of soreness are apparent. The first type is soreness that occurs during the latter stages of or immediately after exercise. This type of soreness is thought to result from high hydrostatic pressure caused by fluid from the blood entering the muscle tissue. The second type of soreness generally appears twelve to forty-eight hours after a strenuous exercise. We have all had the unpleasant experience of waking up the next morning barely able to move after a previous day's exercise. This type of soreness is thought to be the result of small tears in muscle tissue or possible spasms in the muscle brought about by reduced blood supply. Generally muscle soreness after exercise can be limited if there is a good pre- and post-warm-up and stretching. Stretching can also bring some relief from existing pain in the muscle. Easy swimming or cycling can help reduce soreness.

Glossary

Actin
Thin contractile protein in muscle fibers

Agonist
Muscle responsible for movement

Antagonist
Muscle which relaxes to allow agonist to contract

Atrophy
Decrease in the size of muscle tissue

Epimysium
Fibrous connective tissue surrounding skeletal muscle

Fasciculus
Bundles of muscle fibers enclosed by connective tissue which make up a skeletal muscle

Fast Twitch
Fast-twitch Type II muscle fibers physiologically adapted for short-term high intensity exercise

Hyperplasia
An increase in the number of muscle cells

Hypertrophy
Enlargement in muscle size

Ligament
Connective tissue which attaches bone to bone

Muscle Soreness
Muscle pain resulting from chemical or physical changes in the muscle tissue

Myosin
Thick contractile filaments which make up the muscle fibers
Slow Twitch
Slow-twitch Type I muscle fibers physiologically adapted for endurance activity with a high capacity to use oxygen
Tendon
A cord of connective tissue which attaches muscle to bone

Training Concepts

8

Objectives

After studying this chapter you should be able to:

1. Define strength, power and speed.
2. Describe force potential.
3. Describe nerve control of skeletal muscles.
4. Define isotonic, isometric, eccentric, concentric, and isokinetic contraction.

Strength training has finally emerged from the dark ages of ignorance and uncertainty. In recent years a great deal of excellent research has occurred in the areas of muscle cell physiology and muscle training techniques. As a result, a substantial body of knowledge has been established that supports a number of basic muscle training concepts.

Strength, Power, and Speed

There has always been a great deal of interest in the amount of maximal force or strength potential of muscles. *Muscle strength* (the amount of force that can be exerted by a muscle group for one movement or repetition) has always been considered to be an essential basis of athletic skill. Strength training by its nature emphasizes the force component of a movement but not the acceleration component essential in power. Recently, however, new interest has arisen in the maximal rate that a muscle can generate and transfer mechanical energy, which is expressed as power. Power is basically the product of strength and speed (power = force × distance/time). It is obvious from this formula that muscle power is dependent on the interaction of strength and speed. An increase in either force or speed will result in increased power. However, strength will play only a minor role unless the athlete can apply it explosively over a short period of time. The great majority of sports require power and, though strength is an essential ingredient of power, speed must receive special consideration. For example, the strongest football lineman may not necessarily be the best if he doesn't have the speed that allows him to outmaneuver and outleverage his opponent. The quickness of the first step in basketball, changing direction in football, and the explosiveness out of the starting blocks in sprinting also point out the critical interaction between muscle force and speed.

The effects of strength training on muscle speed are not well understood. However, speed training is different from strength training. Strength training requires a high level of resistance that prohibits fast movement. Speed, on the other hand, can best be enhanced by repeatedly practicing the specific movements required in the particular sport skill. Because speed depends upon activating the appropriate neuromuscular pattern involved in a particular skill, it is important to train at velocities of movement similar to or faster than those of the specific sport movement. Speed is defined as strength guided by skill. To increase speed one needs to increase strength and to maintain or increase skill.

Another consideration sometimes overlooked when the emphasis is on strength is that high power efforts typically involve high movement velocities that are coupled with brief contraction time. In rapid movement there is little kinesthetic feedback to the individual regarding the amount of force generated. It is possible that many athletes who train with weights become conditioned to make their best efforts when they can sense the force they are developing. It is tempting to speculate that successful athletes may be those who have learned to use upper motor centers for performing maximum power contractions without relying on kinesthetic feedback or relying on a critical feedback period of short duration.

Strength

An enhanced arousal level and accompanying nerve disinhibition and/or possible neural facilitation are the probable explanations for the unexplained feats of strength performed in emergency situations. In such a situation an individual is capable of achieving his individual maximum level of strength. Significant changes in neural facilitation also occur in the early stages of strength training programs which partly account for rapid increases in strength in these stages.

Neuromuscular Facilitation

A motor unit consists of a motor nerve cell (neuron) that originates in the spinal cord and all the muscle fibers supplied by that neuron. The number of muscle fibers innervated by a single motor nerve varies from a few in some eye muscles to as many as a thousand in the large thigh muscle. All of the muscle fibers within a given unit are of the same fiber type. The muscle fibers are located throughout the muscle and all contract simultaneously when stimulated by the nervous system. Even though our present knowledge of patterns of motor unit activity are still not well understood, it is apparent that different patterns are optimal for different activities.

Force Potential

There are basically three ways in which training overload can enhance the maximal strength of muscles. These are: the number of motor units called into action, the frequency of the nerve impulses, and the coordination of nerve impulses. Increased frequency of nerve impulses results in increased force and decreased frequency in decreased force. The degree of muscle tension is dependent upon the

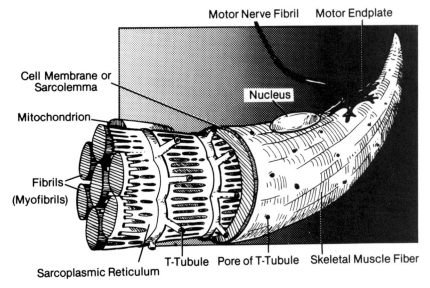

Motor Nerve Fibril   Motor Endplate

Cell Membrane or
Sarcolemma

Nucleus

Mitochondrion

Fibrils
(Myofibrils)

Sarcoplasmic Reticulum   T-Tubule   Pore of T-Tubule   Skeletal Muscle Fiber

Figure 8.1

Nerve impulse transmission. From Jack H. Wilmore and David L. Costill, *Training for Sport and Activity*, 3d ed. Copyright © 1988 Wm. C. Brown Publishers, Dubuque, Iowa. All Rights Reserved. Reprinted by permission.

number and frequency of motor units activated by the central nervous system. The more units recruited, the stronger the maximal contraction. Finally, nerve impulses have to be properly synchronized in order to allow for unified contraction, which is essential for maximum force.

Nerve Impulses and Strength

Both excitatory and inhibitory stimuli descend from the brain to the motor nerves. One explanation for increases in strength is that through training one can learn to decrease the inhibitory impulses from the brain to the muscles, thus allowing for a greater recruitment of force. In other words, physical training may be responsible for various adaptations of the brain and spinal cord. Another factor to consider is that certain muscle groups can be maximally activated through voluntary muscle contraction while others cannot. It may be that those muscles which can be more voluntarily activated receive greater stimulation from the brain. Unfortunately, evidence in this area is somewhat incomplete.

Muscle Cross Section

One of the best indicators of the maximum strength capability of a muscle is its cross sectional area. The larger the cross section, the greater the strength of the muscle and vice versa. This fact is particularly true in isolated muscles where there is an extremely high correlation between cross sectional area and maximal force. However, the relationship is much less in the whole organism than in the isolated muscle. Also, it has been found that increases in strength as a result of training may sometimes be disproportionate to muscle size and due possibly to improved neural facilitation. This observation may explain why women are able to make significant increases in strength with small changes in cross-sectional muscle size.

Muscle Length

There is an optimum length of a muscle at which it can generate its greatest force. Muscles are generally their strongest at a length slightly longer than their normal resting length in their fully extended position. Also, muscles are weaker at shorter and longer lengths than the optimum.

Weight Resistance Methods

As a general rule, a muscle worked close to its maximum capacity will increase in strength. The overload can be applied by a wide variety of weight lifting equipment, free weights, ropes, isokinetic devices, pulleys, etc. Strength improvement is governed primarily by the intensity of the overload and not the method, though certain methods may be more appropriate in some circumstances than others. Isotonics, isometrics, eccentric, and isokinetic contractions are the most widely used techniques for increasing strength and endurance in muscles.

Isotonic Exercise

Isotonic exercise is exercise that is performed against resistance while the load remains constant. The resistance varies with the angle of the joint, for example, lifting free weights (barbells) or weight stacks, such as those used in the universal gym. Free weights are most popular among today's athletes as they feel that the motions are most similar to sport skill movements.

Eccentric Loading

Eccentric loading is sometimes referred to as a negative contraction because the muscle lengthens as it develops tension. An example would be letting yourself down slowly from a chin-up. This type of exercise tends to produce more muscle soreness, possibly due to micro tears in the muscle fibers and tendons, than other techniques. It is not superior to other isotonic methods but is used mainly as a supplement to other training techniques.

Isometric Exercise

An isometric exercise is a contraction performed against a fixed or immovable resistance, where tension is developed in the muscle, but there is no change in the length of the muscle or the angle of the joint. Isometric exercise is also called static contraction. An example would be holding a heavy weight in one position for a fixed amount of time or pushing against a wall.

It appears that with isometric exercise strength development is specific only to the joint angle stimulated during training. As a result, isometric exercise does not increase strength throughout the range of movement. Isometric exercise also may inhibit the ability of the muscle to exert force rapidly, such as is necessary in the shot-put and discus events. In addition, isometric exercise increases pressure in the chest cavity, which results in reduced blood flow to the heart, lungs and brain, along with increased blood pressure. Consequently, isometric exercises are not recommended for individuals with cardiovascular problems. There also may be some decrease in muscular endurance as isometrics restricts peripheral blood flow during the static contraction.

Isokinetic Exercise

An isokinetic exercise is a contraction in which the muscle contracts maximally at a constant speed over a full range of the joint movement against a variable resistance. Isokinetic means equal motion, which is interpreted to mean equal rate of motion or equal speed. An isokinetic contraction can only be accomplished with the use of special equipment, such as a minigym that utilizes "accommodating resistance." In other words, the harder you pull, the harder the gym resists you—the resistance is always related to the applied force.

Isokinetic exercise has become popular because it provides a speed-specific indication of the absolute strength of the muscle group being trained, thus enabling one to more closely replicate some specific athletic skills. The most effective strength gains have come from speeds of approximately sixty degrees (measure of distance) per one second or less. Recent research, however, has indicated that training at fast speeds of movement generally increases strength at all speeds of movement.

Advantages and Disadvantages of Weight-Resistance Programs

Isotonic, isometric, eccentric, and isokinetic exercise all have their advantages and disadvantages. As long as the muscle is overloaded, however, it will gain in strength.

Isotonic Exercise

Advantages

1. It generally produces strength gains throughout the full range of movement.
2. Progress in strength gains is easy to evaluate because of numbered free weights and universal stacks.
3. Strength exercises can be developed to duplicate a variety of sports skills.
4. If free weights are used, balance and symmetry are enhanced.

Disadvantages

1. The equipment is cumbersome.
2. There is a greater potential for accidents.
3. Most strength gains occur at the weakest point of the movement and are not uniform throughout.

Eccentric Exercise

Advantages

1. It is as effective in strength gains as isotonic and isometric.
2. It increases motivation of some individuals who enjoy lifting heavier resistance.
3. It may increase one's skill by lowering resistance slowly.
4. It can duplicate a variety of movements.

Disadvantages

1. It can cause greater post-exercise soreness than other methods.
2. A partner as spotter is needed to lift heavier resistance.

Isometric Exercise

Advantages

1. Little time is required for training.
2. Expensive and cumbersome equipment is not needed.
3. Exercise can be performed anywhere—in home, office, or on vacation.

Disadvantages

1. Strength gains are not produced throughout the full range of movement.
2. Strength gains are difficult to evaluate; that is, no numbered weights or gauges generally are used.
3. It increases the pressure in the chest cavity, causing reduced blood flow to the heart, lungs, and brain.
4. It is not as efficient in producing strength gains as isotonic and isokinetic methods.
5. It is not effective in producing increases in skilled movements.
6. Motivation is difficult to maintain.
7. Muscular endurance may decrease.

Isokinetic Exercise

Advantages

1. It produces maximum resistance through the full range of movement.
2. It increases strength throughout the full range of movement.
3. It may result in less injury and soreness than isometric and isotonic exercise.
4. The uniqueness of the equipment may increase motivation.
5. Strength gains are easy to determine.
6. It is adaptable to specific movement patterns.
7. It permits skill improvement.

Disadvantages

1. The equipment is very expensive with limited availability.
2. Research is still incomplete with regard to motor patterns and force-velocity relationships.
3. Applicability to sport-specific ballistic skills may be limited and may be best for tension skills (i.e. swimming and running).
4. A high level of motivation is required to give full effort to each exercise.

Glossary

Eccentric
Exercise in which the muscle lengthens as it develops tension.

Isokinetic
A contraction in which the muscle contracts maximally at a constant speed over a full range of joint movement against a variable resistance.

Isometric
A contraction performed against a fixed or immovable resistance where tension is developed in the muscle, but there is no change in the length of the muscle or angle of the joint.

Isotonic
Exercise against resistance while the load remains constant, with the resistance varying with the angle of the joint.

Muscle Strength
The amount of force that can be exerted by a muscle group for one movement or repetition.

Power
The product of strength and speed.

Speed
Strength guided by skill.

Advanced Training

9

Objectives

After studying this chapter you should be able to:

1. Describe the pyramid system.
2. Describe super sets.
3. Describe burnouts.
4. Describe partial repetition.
5. Describe circuit training.
6. Describe periodization.
7. Describe forced repetition.
8. Describe negative work.
9. Describe split routine.
10. Describe plyometrics.

Once you have mastered the basic techniques of strength training and have developed a high level of strength and endurance, you may be tempted to enter into advanced training.

No unanimity of opinion exists on the best training system, but generally success in weight training will depend on your progression and quality of work.

The following systems and techniques are commonly used today by advanced weight lifters.

Pyramid System

This is the most popular system for strength and power development. Progression from a low weight to a higher weight with a decreasing number of repetitions is the hallmark of this system. The following is an example of a pyramid system:

Table 9.1   Pyramid System

Set Number	Number of Repetitions	Weight (in lbs)
1	10	155
2	8	185
3	6	205
4	4	225
5	2	245
6	1	255

The athlete may then work his way back down to lower weights and higher repetitions.

Super Sets

This is a system in which the lifter performs one exercise and quickly follows it with another exercise, then rests. The individual works on the two exercises alternately until a desired number of sets has been completed. Adding a third exercise to this routine is called trisets.

Burnouts

In this system, after you complete what is normally your last set, you take some weight off the bar and immediately do an additional set. You continue doing sets with less weight each time and without rest for up to five or six sets or exhaustion.

Partial Repetitions

At the end of the last repetition, usually of the last set of an exercise, when the lifter is unable to perform another full repetition, he or she performs one-half, one-third, or one-fourth of a repetition until these cannot be continued.

Circuit Training

This is a system in which a number of exercise stations are set up and an individual performs one set at each station, then moves to the next station.

These progressive programs can be set up for strength, endurance, cardiovascular endurance or a combination of programs. The number of stations can be as many as fifteen and the rest period in between from thirty seconds to one minute.

Periodization

This is a system of training whereby the individual breaks the calendar year down into training cycles and performs different types of lifting during separate periods of the cycle. The length of the cycle is usually from ten to twelve weeks and is comprised of separate periods of two to four weeks in duration during which the individual focuses upon endurance, strength, power (speed), and rejuvenation (active rest). On a less specific scale athletes use periodization when they follow off-season and in-season training programs.

Forced Repetition

After the last full repetition of the last set the spotter helps the lifter perform another one to three repetitions by assisting the lifter as needed to complete the repetitions.

Negative Work

After the last set has been completed, additional weight is added to the bar and the lifter with the aid of spotters slowly lowers the weight. The spotters then raise the weight and the lifter lowers it again. This process may be repeated for three to five repetitions and several sets.

Split Routine

Rather than performing the entire workout program in one day, many lifters break up their programs into alternate day routines. A lifter may work the upper body on Monday, Wednesday and Friday, and the lower body on Tuesday, Thursday and Saturday. This routine results in more workouts per week but each workout is shorter. Many athletes find that they can perform higher intensity workouts with this method.

Plyometrics

Plyometrics is a procedure whereby a load is placed on a muscle as it is lengthening. Examples include jumping off a box onto the ground and rebounding as quickly as possible. The deceleration and acceleration of body weight provides the overload. Plyometrics are a popular type of exercise for jumpers and sprinters in track and field and is gaining some favor in the throwing events as well. By applying force and velocity in stretching a muscle, plyometrics train the neuromuscular apparatus to respond more forcefully and quickly. An example of upper body plyometrics is to perform repeated push-ups in which you push off the floor, clap your hands together and quickly return your hands to the proper position before you land. This type of push-up requires deceleration of the body on the way down and rapid acceleration on the up phase to reach the necessary height in order to clap your hands.

Caution—This combination of high force and speed produces very significant loads on the muscles, tendons, and ligaments. These structures need to be well conditioned to both force and speed before plyometric exercises are attempted. Proper technique and form are very important in performing these exercises in order to reduce the impact shock and protect the joints and joint structure.

Glossary

Burnout
Continued sets with reduction in resistance until exhaustion.

Circuit Training
A combination of strength and or endurance exercises performed in sequence at various stations.

Forced Repetitions
Performing additional repetitions with assistance when muscle can no longer complete movement.

Negative Work
Exercise in which spotters raise the weight, lifter slowly lowers the weight.

Partial Repetition
Performing an exercise without moving the weight through the complete range of motion at either the beginning of a repetition or at the end of a repetition.

Periodization
Calendar year broken down into various training cycles.

Pyramid System
Progression from low weight to higher weight with decreasing number of repetitions.

Plyometrics
Exercise in which the muscle is loaded suddenly and forced to stretch before the contraction for movement occurs.

Split Routine
A routine in which certain parts of body are worked on one day and other parts on alternate days.

Super Sets
Alternating back and forth between two exercises until the prescribed number of sets are completed.

Exercises

10

Objectives

After studying this chapter you should be able to:

1. Describe a strength exercise for the chest.
2. Describe a strength exercise for the back.
3. Describe a strength exercise for the shoulder.
4. Describe a strength exercise for the trunk.
5. Describe a strength exercise for the hips.
6. Describe a strength exercise for the thighs.
7. Describe a strength exercise for the calf muscles.
8. Describe a flexibility exercise for each major joint.

This chapter provides a selection of the most effective and popular exercises for various body parts. These include exercises with free weights and machines, flexibility exercises, and cardiorespiratory exercise equipment.

The first section includes weight training exercises for chest, back, shoulder, arms (biceps, triceps and forearms), trunk (abdominals and lower back), hips, and thigh and calf.

The second section includes flexibility exercises.

The third section shows cardiorespiratory exercise equipment.

Figure 10.1
Bench press.

Muscles Used:
Primary: Pectoralis Major.
Additional: Anterior Deltoid
Biceps Brachii.
Triceps Brachii.

The weight is lowered to the chest and returned to the starting position. Hands are slightly wider than shoulder width, thumbs should be wrapped around the bar, with feet flat on floor.

Figure 10.2
Inclined dumbbell fly.

Muscles Used:
Same as Bench press, with more emphasis on the upper Pectoralis Major fibers.

Lower the dumbbells to the side with a wide elbow position, then return to starting position.

Figure 10.3
Declined bench press.

Muscles Used:
Primary: Same as Bench press but with more emphasis on lower portion of Pectoralis Major.

The weight is lowered to the chest and returned to the starting position. Hands are slightly wider than shoulder width, thumbs should be wrapped around the bar, with feet flat on floor.

Figure 10.4
Pec Deck Machine.

Muscles Used:
Pectoralis Major with emphasis on the inner/medial fibers.

From the starting position bring your arms together until the machine arms nearly touch, then return to starting position.

Figure 10.5
Bent rowing.

Muscles Used:
Primary: Upper back musculature,
Rhomboid Major and Minor, Teres Major
and Minor.
Additional: Posterior Deltoid Latissimus
Dorsi.

Place feet shoulder width apart. Hands
should be about shoulder width apart with
knees slightly bent. The bar is lifted to the
chest and then lowered. Be careful not to
twist or jerk the lower back. The exercise
can be done with the head resting on a
bench or table to help support the lower
back.

Figure 10.6
Seated pulley rows.

Muscles Used: Same muscles as Bent
Rowing.

Knees are bent and the back is held
straight. The hand grip is brought to the
chest and then returned to the starting
position.

Figure 10.7
Lateral pull down.

Muscles Used: Latissimus Dorsi.

A wide grip is taken on the bar and then the bar is pulled to shoulder level. For heavy resistance a seated position can be used to enable a restraining bar to be placed above the knees in order to keep the body down.

Figure 10.8
Press (Military Press).

Muscles Used:
Primary: Trapezius, Deltoid.
Additional: Supraspinatus, Levator
Scapulae.

Feet are placed flat on the floor
approximately shoulder width apart. The
hand grip is slightly wider than shoulder
width. The bar is pressed overhead and
then returned to the starting position.

In Figure 10.8 a weight rack is used which
provides a safety measure for heavy
weights. When lifting high resistances in
this lift a weight belt may be used to
support the lower back.

If a weight rack is not used, the weight is
brought from a floor resting position up to
the on-shoulder position in what is called
a clean movement.

Figure 10.9
Upright rowing.

Muscles Used:
Primary: Trapezius, Deltoid.
Additional: Supraspinatus, Levator Scapulae.

A close, narrow grip is used. The bar is brought up to just below chin level and returned to the starting position.

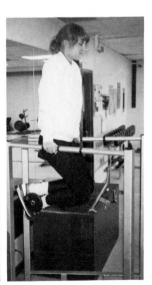

Figure 10.10
Shoulder dips.

Muscles Used:
Primary: Anterior Deltoid Pectoralis Major.
Additional: Triceps Brachii, Biceps Brachii.

This exercise is performed on parallel bars. From the upright position, lower yourself to as low a position as possible, then push up to the upright position. The exercise may be performed with weights held by the feet and legs (see fig. 10.10).

Figure 10.11
Curl.

Muscles Used:
Primary: Biceps Brachii, Brachialis.
Additional: Coracobrachialis,
Brachioradialis, Anterior Deltoid.

Feet and hands shoulder width apart. The bar is brought up to the shoulders and returned to the starting position. Keep your back straight and knees slightly bent to discourage cheating.

 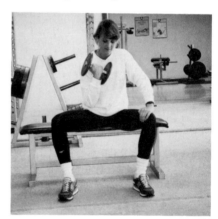

Figure 10.12
Seated alternate dumbbell curls.

Muscles Used: Same as Curl.

Seated position with feet and knees wide apart. The elbow of the lifting arm is in tight to the thigh. The opposite hand rests on the opposite thigh. After the target number of repetitions is achieved, the weight is switched to the other hand.

Figure 10.13
Tricep pullovers.

Muscles Used:
Primary: Triceps Brachii.
Additional: Pectoralis Major, Latissimus Dorsi.
This exercise is especially effective for working the long head of the Triceps.

Lie on a bench with the feet on the bench or flat on the floor. Hold the dumbbell with both hands and bring it up from the floor to a position directly above the head. Return it to near the floor.

Figure 10.14
Seated triceps dumbbell curls.

Muscles Used:
Primary: Triceps Brachii.
Additional: Deltoid.

From a seated position, using one arm at a time, bring the dumbbell down to a position between the shoulder blades (scapulae) and return to the starting position.

Figure 10.15
Tricep pulldowns.

Muscles Used:
Primary: Triceps Brachii.
Additional: Posterior Deltoid, Latissimus Dorsi.

Use a narrow grip. Bring the bar down close to the body to a position in front of the hips with the arms fully extended. Caution against the use of the trunk in an effort to handle more weight.

Figure 10.16
Forearm curls.

Muscles Used:
Primary: Forearm Flexors, Flexor Carpi Radialis, Flexor Carpi Ulnaris.
Additional: Flexor Digitorum Profundus, Flexor Digitorum Superficialis.

Rest the forearms on the thighs for support. Hold the bar with a palm-up grip, and flex the hands and wrist upwards. A reverse, palm-down grip can be used to perform a reversed forearm curl for development of the posterior forearm muscles.

Figure 10.17
Bent-knee sit-ups.

Muscles Used:
Primary: Rectus Abdominis.
Additional: Internal Obliques, External Obliques, Transverse Abdominis.

Start flat on the floor with feet secured under a dresser, pads, or sit-up board. A spotter also can hold your feet. Bend knees to at least a ninety degree angle to place less stress on the lower back. Straight-up sit-ups work primarily the rectus abdominis while twisting sit-ups add work for the oblique muscles.

Figure 10.18
Crunches.

Muscles Used: Same as Bent-Knee Sit-ups.

Place legs on a bench. Start this sit-up flat on the floor and bring torso up until elbows touch the knees.

Figure 10.19
Alternate knee touching sit-ups.

Muscles Used: Abdominal Group.

Starting flat on the floor, raise upward and touch your elbow to your opposite knee. Repeat for the opposite elbow and knee. This exercise is excellent for oblique development.

a

b

Figure 10.20
(a) Sit-ups on an incline bench
(b) Sit-ups with weights.

Muscles Used: Abdominal Group.

Start flat on the floor and move to a fully trunk upright position.

The use of weights adds resistance for greater strength development.

Figure 10.21
Side bend with dumbbell.

Muscles Used:
Primary: Transverse Abdominis.
Additional: Internal Obliques, External Obliques.

From an upright standing position, bend to the side, stretching the opposite side. Try to concentrate on isolating the musculature to slowly return to the upright position.

Be careful not to use too heavy a weight as this area will increase in size.

Figure 10.22
Seated bar twists.

Muscles Used:
Primary: Transverse Abdominis.
Additional: Internal Oblique, External
Oblique.

From a seated or standing position with a bar or broomstick on your shoulders and your hands spread wide and grasping the bar, twist to one side and reverse twist to the other.

Try to isolate the abdominal muscles while performing this exercise.

a

b

c

Figure 10.23
(a & b) Back hyperextension (c) with weights.

Muscles Used:
Primary: Erector Spinal Group.

Using a back hyperextension machine, start from the down (flexed) position and move upward into a hyperextended position. This exercise can be performed with light weights to build greater strength. Take care, however, as the lower back muscles are subject to spasms. Use only light weights.

a   b

c

Figure 10.24
(a & b) Half squat (c) full squat.

Muscles Used:
Primary: Gluteals, Quadriceps, Hamstrings.
Full squats involve more Gluteal use.

The safest way to perform squats is to use a squat rack, as shown in figure 10.24. Starting from an upright position with the bar on your shoulders, bend at the knees and slightly lower yourself to a position of a ninety degree angle between your thigh and leg. This is a half squat. In the full squat, lower yourself to a fully lowered position. Full squats put great stress on the knees and can produce injuries in susceptible individuals. Take special care while doing full squats. We recommend half squats.

Figure 10.25

Leg press.

Muscles Used:
Primary: Quadriceps.
Additional: Hamstrings, Gluteals.

Adjust the seat so that there is a ninety degree angle or less at the knees. From this position press until legs are extended.

Figure 10.26

Hip flexion.

Muscles Used:
Primary: Ileopsoas.
Additional: Rectus Femoris, Quadriceps Group.

Face away from the weight pulley. Extend your leg behind you, then bring the leg forward.

Figure 10.27
Four-way hip extension.

Muscles Used:
Primary: Gluteals.
Additional: Hamstrings.

Place your leg in front of you, then bring your leg backwards into a hyperextended position behind you.

Figure 10.28
Hip adduction.

Muscles Used:
Primary: Adductor Group (Groin Muscles).

Stand with legs wide apart, then bring one leg inward and across in front of the support leg.

Figure 10.29
Hip abduction.

Muscles Used:
Primary: Gluteus Medius, and Minimus.
Additional: Tensor Fascia Latae.

From a position slightly in front of the support leg, move the leg outward to the side.

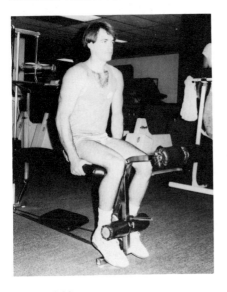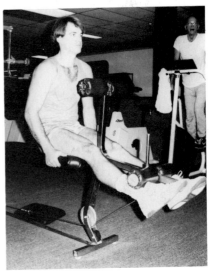

Figure 10.30
Leg extension.

Muscles Used: Quadriceps.

Move the legs from a flex position to an extended position, pause momentarily, and return. Start with your legs at a right angle and pause with your legs straight.

Figure 10.31
Leg flexion.

Muscles used:
Primary: Hamstrings (semitendinosus, Semimembrinosus, Biceps Femoris).

Lying prone on the bench with your heels behind the pads, flex the legs and bring your heels toward your buttocks.

Figure 10.32
Toe raise.

Muscle Used:
Primary: Posterior Calf groups, Gastrocnemius, Soleus.
Additional: Tibialis Posterior.

Starting from a position in which your heels are lower than your forefeet, press upwards using the calf muscles until you are standing on your toes.

Figure 10.33
Seated toe raises.

Muscles Used: Same as toe raise.

Slide your feet halfway down the foot platform so that the balls of your feet are on the platform but your heels are off. Press forward and back from a toes-back to a toes-forward position.

Figure 10.34
Seated trunk twist.

In a seated position extend one leg and bend the opposite leg with the foot resting flat next to the knee. Place opposite hand on extended leg just below knee and twist trunk toward extended leg. Hold ten seconds and repeat five times. Then alternate with other leg.

Figure 10.35
Shoulder stretch.

Place both hands shoulder width apart on a ledge or stationary bar. Bend knees slightly and let upper body drop down. Adjust height of hands and degree of knee bend to increase or decrease stretch. Hold ten seconds. Repeat five times.

Figure 10.36
Hyperextended shoulder stretch.

Stand with your feet slightly apart. Grasp your hands behind your back and raise your arms. Hold ten seconds. Repeat six times.

Figure 10.37
Standing side and shoulder stretch.

With your feet shoulder width apart and arms folded behind head, bend your trunk to the side. Hold position ten seconds, then alternate to the other side. Repeat five times.

Figure 10.38
Hip flexor stretch.

Move one leg forward until knee of front leg is directly over ankle. Rest back knee on floor. Without changing leg position, lower front hip downward to create stretch. Hold ten seconds. Repeat five times. Change leg position and repeat.

Figure 10.39
Hip extensor stretch.

Lie on your back with both legs straight. Grasp one leg just below the knee and pull the knee to your chest. Hold ten seconds, then alternate with the other leg. Repeat five times.

Figure 10.40
Exercise bicycle.

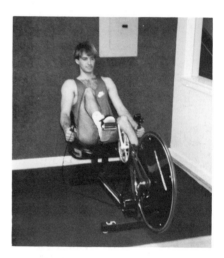

Figure 10.41
Recumbant exercise bicycle.

Figure 10.42
Computerized exercise bicycle.

Figure 10.43
Treadmill.

Figure 10.44
Stair climbing machine.

Figure 10.45
Cross-country skiing machine.

Figure 10.46
Arm ergometer.

Figure 10.47
Versi-climber.

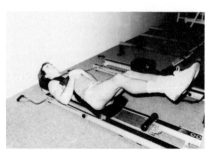

Figure 10.48
Plyometric exercise for lower extremity.

Women and Weight Training

11

Objectives

After studying this chapter you should be able to:

1. Describe the effect of strength training on women.
2. Describe the physical differences between men and women that are significant in strength training.
3. Define amenorrhea.
4. Describe exercise guidelines for pregnancy.

Female participation in physical activities has increased markedly over the past few years as outdated social mores regarding women's involvement in exercise and sport have changed.

Increasingly, more and more women are lifting weights. To those of us who have enjoyed the benefits of weight training, the increase in women's weight training is not at all surprising. Having known the benefits for years, we realize that as women began to lift they too would enjoy and desire the benefits as well.

One reason why the increase has been so dramatic is that women have found that through weight training they become stronger. Strength builds confidence. Being stronger improves your confidence, your self-image and your concept of what goals can be achieved. In few, if any, athletic endeavors are these experiences so quickly enjoyed, dramatic in effect, and repeatedly reinforced.

Let's look at some special training considerations for women and their impact on weight training.

Physiology

Men's and women's response to cardiorespiratory training is nearly identical. When it comes to skeletal-muscular training, however, some differences in response to training do occur. These differences are not a function of muscle physiology but rather hormonal influences.

Women have a smaller amount of muscle mass and greater amount of subcutaneous fat stores that tend to lessen muscle definition. Women on average have about three-quarters the amount of absolute strength of males, however, their percentage of strength increases as a result of training are approximately the same. Also, female body builders have dramatically high lean to fat ratios in comparison to other female athletes.

Males have a much higher level of testosterone circulating within their bodies. This male sex hormone is also present in women but in significantly lesser amounts. The influence of testosterone on skeletal muscles is, with the aid of training, to increase muscle mass. Because women have lower levels of testosterone, the increase in muscle mass (hypertrophy) they experience with weight training is significantly less. Very few women increase dramatically in muscle mass as a result of weight training. Those that do have an unusually high level of testosterone in their systems or may be using anabolic steroids (see chapter 15).

Most women respond to weight training by increasing their strength, endurance, and muscle tone, but they do so without the significant increases in muscle mass that men experience. Very few women need to worry about becoming "too big" or "masculinized" as a result of weight training. However, with exceptional overload and volume they may increase muscle mass.

If a woman chooses to use anabolic steroids to raise her testosterone level, she will respond to training in the same manner as a man and will produce muscle mass increases in a similar fashion. There are, however, side effects to using anabolic steroids that may be unacceptable to her such as deepening voice, increase in body hair, acne, high blood pressure, and other problems (see chapter 15).

Physical Differences

The bone structure of the female pelvic girdle is wider than a male's to facilitate the birthing process. Women's knees, however, are approximately the same distance apart as a man's. This combination results in a greater convergence angle and stress, and, thus, a greater likelihood that women will experience knee problems when performing squats, particularly deep or full squats. Women should gradually increase the resistance they use in these lifts to prevent this problem.

Percentage of Body Fat

Women have a higher percentage of body fat than men. This is true in the general population (men, 12 to 17; women, 19 to 24) as well as in comparing male and female athletes (men, 4 to 10 percent; women, 10 to 14 percent). Exercise can reduce body fat and this reduction occurs without sex discrimination. Women often, however, start with a higher percentage and retain a higher percentage even when highly trained (as compared to a highly trained male).

Menstruation

The cause of exercise amenorrhea (cessation of menstruation) is still unknown. However, a number of theories exist including increased testosterone and decreased ovarian function, loss of body fat, and active pituitary functioning. Presently, there is a strong indication that a change in hypothalamic functioning may be responsible. Sufficient calcium replacement is essential for individuals encountering amenorrhea.

Most women who cease menstruation appear to suffer no physiological problems, but the long-term effects are unknown. If amenorrhea does occur, cutting back on training, eliminating stress, and raising the percentage of body fat above ten percent are recommended.

Exercise Guidelines for Pregnancy

1. Exercise intensity should not go beyond a seventy percent maximum effort level.
2. Exercise should be stopped if there is any pain or bleeding.
3. Adequate intakes of iron, calcium, and vitamins should be ensured before and during pregnancy.
4. Avoid bouncing, jarring, and twisting activities that put your abdomen in jeopardy.
5. If you feel tired or experience discomfort, stop and rest.
6. You should not exercise so intensely that you are unable to talk.
7. Don't exercise while lying on your back after fourth month. This can block blood supply to the uterus and depress fetal heart rate. If you need to rest, lie on your side.
8. Don't exercise vigorously in hot weather, (core body temperature should not go above 101 degrees Fahrenheit).
9. Drink plenty of water before, during, and after exercise.
10. Your exercise program should be started well in advance of your pregnancy.

If a pregnant woman has medical problems, disease or other complications, she should seek advice from an obstetrician before undertaking a rigorous physical exercise program. Rhythmic, moderate activity is well advised and safe for both mother and fetus.

Osteoporosis

A significant number of older women suffer from a decrease in bone density (osteoporosis) after menopause. Presently sixty-seven percent of women over age sixty-five are expected to suffer from a hip fracture and/or a fractured vertebrae due to osteoporosis. Recent studies have demonstrated that simply adding increased calcium to one's diet does little if anything to slow down the process. Some success has been found by combining increased calcium intake with an aerobic exercise program. Weight training with light weights supplemented with the proper diet may prove to be an answer as training has been shown to increase bone density in all age groups regardless of gender.

Glossary

Amenorrhea

Abnormal cessation of menstruation.

Anabolic Steroids

Synthetic hormones that are similar to the male hormone testosterone.

Hypothalamus

Portion of brain controlling hormonal functioning among many other responsibilities.

Menopause

The natural cessation of menstruation occurring near age fifty.

Osteoporosis

A loss in bone materials and density producing brittleness and softness of the bone.

Cardiorespiratory Fitness

12

Objectives

After studying this chapter you should be able to:

1. Describe cardiorespiratory fitness.
2. Describe the target heart rate method.
3. Define aerobic and anaerobic exercise.
4. Describe intensity, duration and frequency of cardiorespiratory training.
5. Define cooling down.
6. Describe the American College of Sports Medicine Recommendations of Exercise.

The body's ability to deliver oxygen and nutrients rapidly and efficiently to all vital organs such as the heart, nervous system and working muscles is the basis of cardiorespiratory endurance. A well-conditioned heart and efficient respiratory system are essential to a high level of physical fitness. Table 12.1 lists the benefits of cardiorespiratory training on the body.

Maximum Oxygen Uptake

The maximum amount of oxygen utilized by the cells during strenuous exercise per unit of time is referred to as maximum oxygen uptake. Maximum oxygen uptake is the most accurate indicator of cardiorespiratory fitness.

Cardiorespiratory Endurance

Cardiorespiratory endurance is the body's ability to sustain prolonged vigorous exercise. Muscular endurance, though partly dependent on the cardiorespiratory system, refers to the ability of a muscle or muscle group to sustain prolonged movement. Muscular endurance is related to muscular strength and is specific to the muscles that are being exercised.

Table 12.1 Benefits of Cardiorespiratory Training

Cardiorespiratory Training Increases	Cardiorespiratory Training Produces	Cardiorespiratory Training Decreases
Tolerance to stress	Lower resting heart rate	Obesity-adiposity
Arterial oxygen content	Physical conditioning of muscles	Arterial blood pressure
Electron transport activity	Greater oxygen utilization	Heart rate
Efficiency of the heart	Greater stroke volume	Vulnerability to dysrhythmias
Blood vessel size		Stress response
Efficiency of blood circulation	Lower heart rate for submaximal work	Need of heart muscle for oxygen

Aerobic—Anaerobic

All-out exercises lasting two minutes or less without stopping are referred to as anaerobic exercises (without oxygen). Such exercises as sprinting, tennis, handball and weight lifting are examples of anaerobic exercises. For all-around physical fitness anaerobic exercise should be accompanied by continuous vigorous exercise lasting beyond two minutes such as jogging, cycling, and swimming, which train the aerobic system (with oxygen). It is important to do aerobic training before participating in anaerobic activities such as strength training.

Figure 12.1 shows the relative amounts of aerobic versus anaerobic fitness required in different sport activities.

Training Effect

Monitoring your heart rate is a very effective way of determining exercise intensity. This approach is referred to as the threshold effect or training heart rate effect. Research by Karvonen found that a training level of seventy percent of your maximum heart rate, approximately sixty percent of your maximum oxygen uptake level, is considered to be a minimal level of intensity, necessary to increase cardiovascular endurance.

Determining your target heart rate is relatively simple. First you determine your maximum heart rate by subtracting your age from 220. This method is not an exact measure because the formula predicts rather than assesses as a result; there is a possibility of a ten beat per minute error. Next subtract your resting pulse rate from your predicted maximum heart rate, then multiply the difference by seventy percent. Add this product to your resting heart rate; the result will give you your target heart rate level. The resting heart rate is determined by taking your pulse in the morning before you get out of bed. Because of daily fluctuations you should average this figure for three to five days.

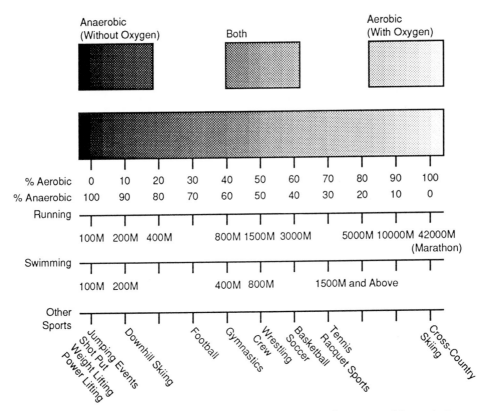

In the running and swimming events, researchers generally agree that at around three minutes (until about seven or eight minutes) there are relatively equal requirements in both the aerobic and anaerobic pathways for muscle energetics.

Figure 12.1
Relative amounts of anaerobic versus aerobic fitness required in different sport activities. From *Aerobic Weight Training* by Frederick C. Hatfield, Ph.D. Copyright © 1985 Contemporary Books, Inc. Reprinted by permission of Contemporary Books, Inc.

The following is an example of determining the target heart rate level for a twenty-year-old individual with a resting heart rate of seventy beats per minute: $220 - 20 = 200$ beats per minute (maximum heart rate) where 20 is the individual's age.

$200 - 70 = 130$ (70 is the resting heart rate in this example)

$130 \times .70 = 91$ (.70 is the desired intensity)

$91 + 70 = 161$ beats per minute where 70 is the resting heart rate

The target heart rate level in this example is 161 beats per minute.

Three basic principles are important to insure proper cardiovascular training effects: intensity, duration and frequency.

Intensity

For a training effect to occur in the cardiovascular and muscular system, the exercise program must consist of activities that produce an overload on these systems. For cardiovascular training the threshold level is seventy percent of your maximum heart rate, as previously outlined. A threshold level of sixty percent is used for post-heart attack victims, obese persons, or persons with a history of sedentary living.

Duration

The length of your exercise will depend primarily on the intensity of the exercise and your long-range goals. Beginners should start at a minimum of ten minutes per exercise period and increase at a rate of two minutes per week up to thirty minutes.

Frequency

To become fit aerobically requires a minimum of three workout sessions per week. Greater results will be achieved with more sessions, but three sessions per week will produce significant increases in cardiovascular conditioning (table 12.2). These three workouts should be spaced evenly through the week to avoid long periods of non-activity. A typical schedule is as follows:

3 day schedule
RUN–M–W–F

5 day schedule
RUN M–W–F   or   RUN T–Th–Sat
BIKE T–Th   BIKE Sun–F

7 day schedule
RUN M–W–F
BIKE T–Th–Sat
SWIM Sun

Table 12.2   Sequence and Time Ranges for Basic Fitness Program

Stage	Duration	Activity
Warm-up, Flexibility	10–15 minutes	Walking, Slow Jogging
Aerobic Exercise	20–40 minutes	Bicycling, Walking, Jogging, Swimming
Cool-down	8–10 minutes	Walking, Stretching

Cooling Down

You should continue to exercise at a low intensity (stretching and walking eight to ten minutes) following a rigorous workout. This step will allow your body to adjust to a resting state. Cooling down prevents the blood from pooling in the lower extremities, which could reduce the amount of blood returning to the heart and disrupt the cardiac cycle. Cooling down also helps reduce muscle soreness, dizziness, and the amount of biochemical fatigue products in the blood.

Circuit Training

Circuit training involves a combination of strength and endurance exercises performed in sequence at various exercise stations. This extremely efficient technique can be specifically designed for a variety of different sports activities. For example, the circuit can emphasize strength, muscular endurance, cardiovascular activities, or a combination of all three. Table 12.3 presents an example of a muscular strength, muscular endurance, and cardiovascular circuit training program. See appendix E for the Universal super circuit.

Exercise Prescription

The American College of Sports Medicine Recommendations:
The American College of Sports Medicine makes the following recommendations for the quantity and quality of training for developing and maintaining cardiorespiratory fitness and body composition in the healthy adult:

1. Frequency of training: three to five days per week.
2. Intensity of training: sixty percent to ninety percent of maximum heart rate.

Table 12.3 Muscle Strength and Cardiovascular Circuit-Training Program

Duration	Ten weeks
Frequency	Three days per week
Circuits/session	Circuit A: 3; Circuit B: 2
Time/circuit	Circuit A: 7½ min; Circuit B: 15 min
Total time/session	Circuit A: 22½ min; Circuit B: 30 min
Load	40 to 55 percent of 1 RM
Repetitions	As many as possible in thirty seconds
Rest	Fifteen seconds between stations

	Muscle Strength and Endurance		Cardiovascular
	Circuit A		Circuit B
Station	Exercise	Station	Exercise
1	Bench press	1	Running (440 yd)
2	Bent-knee sit-ups	2	Push-ups or pull-ups
3	Knee (leg) extension	3	Bent-knee sit-ups
4	Pulldown-lat machine	4	Vertical jumps
5	Back hyperextension	5	Standing (overhead) press
6	Standing (overhead) press	6	Bicycling (3 min)
7	Dead lift	7	Hip stretch
8	Arm curl	8	Rope jumping (1 min)
9	Leg curl (knee flexion)	9	Bent-over rowing
10	Upright rowing	10	Hamstring stretch
		11	Upright rowing
		12	Running (660 yd)

Source: *Sports Psychology*, by Edward L. Fox. Copyright © 1979 by Saunders College Publishing/Holt Rinehart and Winston. Reprinted by permission of CBS College Publishing.

3. Duration of training: fifteen to sixty minutes of continuous aerobic activity. Duration is dependent on the intensity of the activity, thus lower intensity activity should be conducted over a longer period of time. Because of the importance of the total fitness effect and the fact that it is more readily attained in longer duration programs, and because of the potential hazards and compliance problems associated with high intensity activity, lower to moderate intensity activity of longer duration is recommended for the nonathletic adult.

4. Mode of activity: Any activity that uses large muscle groups, that can be maintained continuously and is rhythmical and aerobic in nature, e.g. running, jogging, walking, hiking, swimming, skating, bicycling, rowing, cross-country skiing, rope skipping, and various endurance game activities.

Glossary

Aerobic
Continuous vigorous exercise of long duration, such as jogging, long-distance swimming, and cycling that utilizes large amounts of oxygen.

Anaerobic
All-out exercise lasting one to two minutes or less, such as weight lifting, sprinting, handball, and squash, performed in the absence of oxygen.

Cooling Down
Continuation of exercise at a low intensity following a vigorous workout which allows the body to adjust to a resting state.

Duration
Amount of time utilized for each exercise bout.

Frequency
Number of exercise bouts per week.

Intensity
The level of physiological stress on the body during exercise.

Target Heart Rate
The proper intensity level of an endurance training program, approximately seventy to eighty-five percent of maximum heart rate.

Injuries

13

Objectives

After studying this chapter you should be able to:

1. Describe the major reasons for injury in strength training.
2. Define muscle balance, positioning.
3. Describe important safety procedures.
4. Describe common injuries, prevention, and treatment.

Many of the injuries that occur during strength training are avoidable. A number of individuals are injured because they take unnecessary risks such as trying to lift too much weight, use incorrect techniques, or are avoiding safety guidelines. They may be unaware of how easily they can injure themselves. An injury can force you to stop your program or cut back until you recover. The best way to insure steady progress is to avoid injury.

Weight training, because it places great stress on muscles, tendons and ligaments, is an activity in which minor injuries may occur. Most, however, can be avoided if some simple rules are followed.

1. Lift Progressively.
   Start with a light weight and progressively add resistance with each set. Do not start with your heaviest set first as the muscles and tendons are not prepared for such sudden exertion.
2. Muscle Balance.
   You should exercise opposite muscle groups (prime mover and antagonist) in your workout to insure proper muscle balance.
3. Positioning.
   Proper positioning is important in maintaining the correct alignment of the skeletal system and in positioning the exercised muscles for maximum force development.
4. Lift Safely.
   Review chapter 3.
5. Equipment.
   Always use the proper equipment. Review chapter 3.

6. Overtraining.

The most common cause of injury to lifters is training error. For the beginner it is doing too much too soon, resulting in overfatiguing the muscle, with an inadequate rest and rehabilitation interval. The muscles respond fairly rapidly to the increased demand placed upon them with a lifting program. Tendons and ligaments, however, take significantly longer to adapt to the added stress and will require a more progressive adaptation period if injury is to be avoided.

The key to avoiding overtraining is to make sure you have adequate rest. The rest period is when the muscle recovers and when the gains in strength and endurance occur. You need to listen to your body and adapt the intensity and duration of your exercise program to the needs and ability of your body to recover. There will be times when the best workout you could have is a light workout or no workout at all.

One of the first signs of overtraining is mental staleness. If rest is insufficient in either quality or quantity, then often sickness such as colds or flu occurs.

A common progression is:

1. staleness or slump
2. sickness
3. injury

If you learn to listen to your body, 2 and 3 can be avoided.

Common Injuries

Injuries may also result from the overuse of and lack of rest for the muscles and tendons. The belly of the muscle contains the contractile elements and is where the work of the muscle is performed. The tendons are tough fibers that connect the muscle to the bones.

Lifting injuries can be classified into several groups:

1. tendinitis
2. strains and sprains
3. bursitis
4. dislocations and fractures

Tendinitis

Tendinitis is an inflammation of the tendon and is characterized by swelling and tenderness. It is usually caused by a repeated irritation to an area. This injury is most common when many repetitions of a lift are performed. Common sites for tendinitis are the Achilles tendon in the back of the heel, the patella tendon of the knee, tendons in the shoulder and elbows, and also tendons in the wrist and hand.

Strains and Sprains

A strain is a tear in the muscle and/or tendon. Strains can occur when the muscle is not warmed up properly, a twisting or jerking occurs during the lift, significant force is applied too rapidly (such as in raising or lowering the weight too quickly), or when a previously injured muscle is returned to heavy exercise without adequate rehabilitation.

A sprain is a tear in a ligament. Ligaments are structures which hold the bones together such as those in the knee and ankle. The same circumstances that were listed as causing strains can also cause sprains.

Strains and sprains are classified by degrees:

First degree—tearing of a few fibers resulting in mild tenderness and slight swelling.

Second degree—partial disruption of the involved tissues causing more tenderness and swelling.

Third degree—complete tearing of the tissue resulting in significant pain and swelling. The joint may be difficult to move and/or the torn muscle may exhibit a bulge.

Strains and sprains are the most common type of lifting injuries and occur most often in the following areas:

Strains

1. chest and back muscles (shoulder girdle)
2. arm muscles (shoulder girdle)
3. hamstrings
4. quadriceps

Sprains

1. knee
2. wrist
3. ankle

Bursitis

Another common injury in lifters is bursitis. Bursitis is an inflammation of a bursa which is a sac that contains fluid. This sac is strategically located in or near joints to assist in the joint or tendon movement. Sometimes the sac becomes irritated from abrasion or gets pinched during a joint movement resulting in inflammation, tenderness and pain. The shoulder is the most common site of bursitis for lifters, with bursitis in the knees, hips and elbows as the next most common sites.

Dislocation and Fractures

A dislocation is a separation of the joint surface which can be either partial or complete. The shoulder, elbow, wrist, knee and vertebrae are the most common sites for this injury. In other sports these usually occur by trauma such as a collision in football or a fall in gymnastics. In weight training they can occur when incorrect alignment of a body part occurs during the lift, such as twisting the neck or back while lifting. Dislocation can also occur as a result of a severe sprain or strain that occurs during the lift. Some people, because of their joint structure, are susceptible to dislocation and should exercise caution. Have spotters and insure correct body position. Dislocation usually involves significant pain and lack of mobility as well as swelling and tissue damage.

Fractures are much less common in lifting than in other sports, but they do occur. The two most common sites are the wrist and feet. The overhead lifts such as the snatch and the clean-and-press place significant stress on the wrist joint and can cause a partial crack or complete break in the bones. This causes significant swelling and pain. The other lifting related fractures occur as hairline cracks in the bones of the feet. These are sometimes referred to as fatigue fractures as they usually result from high levels of stress without adequate rest in between periods of exercise. These fatigue fractures exhibit tenderness and swelling.

Most athletes will sustain some injuries during their careers. Fortunately, most of these will be minor and with a little knowledge and care can be self-treated. The key is to learn what injuries you can treat and which ones need medical attention. Much of this awareness is developed by listening to your body.

The following guidelines are recommended in assessing whether or not to seek medical assistance. If the following conditions exist you should seek assistance from an athletic trainer, nurse practitioner, physical therapist and/or a physician.

1. pain that is severe or persists
2. inability to move the injured body part
3. the injury does not appear to be healing

The following procedures should be followed immediately after an injury such as strains, sprains, and/or tendinitis or bursitis.

R. I. C. E.
- Rest
- Ice
- Compression
- Elevation

Using this regime will help relieve pain, control inflammation, and start the healing process. Let's examine each briefly.

Healing

Rest

In severe strains, sprains, bursitis, tendinitis and in all fractures, rest is required, and prolonged rest may be essential to recovery. Your physician should be your guide.

In less severe cases, however, complete rest may not be required. Within a few days of an injury the tissues begin to repair themselves. Proper rehabilitation exercises can aid in the repair by flushing away the injury produced by-products from the tissue and by bringing blood and nutrients to the area. Movement will help restore the functional ability of the muscle and allow for a quicker return to your sport. Allow the pain level and type of pain to be your guide. If the pain is sharp, throbbing and/or very severe then exercise or movement is not indicated. If, however, there is only minor pain, then movement may aid the healing process.

Ice

Ice is important because it reduces the pain and swelling by constricting blood and lymph vessels. Ice should be placed on the injured area as soon as possible after the injury. Ice should be applied for about thirty minutes on a schedule of on for five minutes, off for five minutes, on again for five minutes, etc.

Compression

Wrapping the injured part with an elastic bandage will compress the area and limit swelling. Be careful not to wrap the part too tightly as the blood supply will be cut off. If the part becomes numb and/or turns blue then the wrapping is too tight. The wrapping should remain on for twenty to thirty minutes then released for fifteen minutes to insure adequate circulation. This process may be repeated.

Elevation

Elevating the body part helps drain excess fluid from the area and along with compression can help limit muscular bleeding and swelling. It may be advisable to elevate the part while sleeping.

Other Remedies

Aspirin and Ibuprofen

Aspirin is a powerful anti-inflammatory agent and can be effective in reducing swelling and relieving pain. If you experience stomach upset with aspirin you can try buffered aspirin (such as Bufferin). Non-aspirin pain relievers that contain acetaminophen such as Tylenol can reduce pain but are not thought to diminish inflammation. Ibuprofen can be purchased over-the-counter under the names Advil and Pamprin.

Cortisone, Butazone

These anti-inflammatory agents are prescription drugs and should only be prescribed and administered by a physician and are usually reserved for severe cases.

Heat

Heat such as hot baths, analgesic balm, and heating pads can be helpful in aiding healing but should not be used on an injury until swelling is eliminated or significantly reduced. The rule of thumb is ice for twenty-four to forty-eight hours and then heat if the swelling has been eliminated.

Rehabilitation

You should begin gently range of motion exercises as soon as you can comfortably do so, unless your doctor recommends you not do so. The sooner you begin to use the muscles, the faster you will recover. Moderation is the key! Excessive pain means you are overdoing it!

If you have consulted a physician, athletic trainer or physical therapist, ask him or her to recommend rehabilitation exercises.

Try to learn something from each injury. Some injuries are due to accidents, such as dropping a weight on your foot. In this case all you might learn is that you need to be more careful, pay better attention to detail, or refrain from lifting weights when you are not mentally involved in the activity.

For other injuries, however, you should try to determine:

1. What is the injury? (medical personnel can help you if your anatomy background is weak).
2. What caused the injury?
3. How you can avoid such an injury?

If you answer these questions, you will be better able to prevent injuries in the future.

THE FAR SIDE   By GARY LARSON

Unbeknownst to most historians, Einstein started down the road of professional basketball before an ankle injury diverted him into science.

Glossary

Bursitis
Inflammation of the bursae sac.

Dislocation
Separation of a joint surface.

Muscle Balance
Procedure where opposite muscle groups are exercised to insure proper muscle balance.

Sprain
An injury to the ligament.

Strain
An injury to the muscle or tendon.

Tendinitis
Inflammation of the tendon.

Nutrition

14

Objectives

After studying this chapter you should be able to:

1. Define and describe major nutritional constituents; carbohydrates, fats, proteins, vitamins, minerals, and water.
2. Describe the energy system for muscle contraction.
3. Describe criteria for diet rating.
4. Describe weight loss and weight gain procedures.

Nutritional Concepts

Your dietary needs for strength training or other physically active programs are not very different from those recommended for all healthy individuals. Rigorous exercise programs, however, require more energy expenditure than a sedentary life-style. As a result you may need to consume additional calories; the exact amount will depend on the intensity of training, your age, sex, body composition, and your present fitness level. See table 14.1 for a general estimation of your caloric needs. A diet that is deficient in the basic nutritional requirements will interfere with your strength training goals by producing early fatigue, reducing your performance level and in some cases producing physical deterioration. On the other hand there is no evidence that taking of additional dietary supplements (vitamins, protein, amino acids, etc.) will increase performance levels. In fact, large doses of some supplements such as fat-soluble vitamins may be detrimental to your health.

Nutritional Requirements

The major nutritional requirements are carbohydrates, protein, fats, minerals, vitamins, and water.

Table 14.1 Daily Caloric Needs (Determined by Multiplying Body Weight in Pounds with the Appropriate Number Relating to Activity Level).

Physical Activity	Women	Men
Sedentary	14	16
Moderately active	18	21
Active	22	26

Carbohydrates

Carbohydrates are chemical compounds containing carbon, hydrogen, and oxygen. Examples are starches, grain products, fruits, vegetables, sugars, and milk. Carbohydrates are the most efficient fuel for the body as they are most easily broken down. They should supply fifty-five to sixty percent of daily calories for the average person and sixty to eighty percent for endurance athletes. No more than ten percent of your total calories should come from simple carbohydrates (sugars). The remaining carbohydrates should be complex carbohydrates (starch). Carbohydrates can increase energy reserves (glycogen) in muscles and liver, thus prolonging the time before exhaustion during vigorous exercise.

Proteins

The main function of protein is the building and repair of tissue. It is an energy source only when fats and carbohydrates are not available. Excellent sources of protein are eggs, meat, fish, poultry, dried beans, peas, nuts, milk, and cheese. Protein needs of sedentary and most active people are about the same. The adult requirements are approximately twelve percent of total calories. The Food and Nutrition Board recommends 0.8 grams of protein per kilogram of body weight. Protein supplements are unnecessary and expensive. Excess protein will not build muscles, only exercise will. Extra protein is broken down and stored as fat.

Fats

Fats belong to a class of compounds called lipids and supply energy and promote absorption of fat-soluble vitamins. They provide the primary fuel for prolonged endurance type exercise. Less than thirty percent of your daily calories should come from fat and less than ten percent from saturated fat. Avoid fatty foods before exercise as they require three to four hours to digest. Do not confuse body fat and dietary fat. Body fat is the stored form of excess caloric intake in either protein, carbohydrate or fat.

Table 14.2 Current, Recommended, and High-Energy Nutritional Allowances

	Current	Recommended by American Heart Association	Recommended for High-Energy Needs
Fats	42%	30%	10 to 20%
Protein	12%	12%	10 to 12%
Complex carbohydrates	22%	48%	60 to 80%
Sugar	24%	10%	5 to 10%

Vitamins

Vitamins' main function is the metabolism of carbohydrates, proteins, and fats to produce energy. These organic compounds are needed in only small amounts by the body.

Individuals involved in vigorous physical activity do not require supplementary vitamins. If your caloric intake comes from a varied balanced diet high in complex carbohydrates, it should provide all the vitamins you need. Contrary to popular belief, vitamins do not provide energy or build muscle. There is no evidence of any vitamin improving physical performance.

Minerals

Minerals regulate body processes, maintain body tissue, and aid in metabolism. A varied diet generally provides enough minerals for active people with the possible exception of iron for women. Women should also consume at least 1000 milligrams of calcium per day to protect against the onset of osteoporosis. Losses of sodium and potassium through perspiration are minimal during exercise and are usually replenished by a normal diet. Salt tablets are not necessary and may be detrimental. Table 14.2 shows current and recommended nutritional allowances, as well as nutritional allowances recommended for the high energy needs of vigorous physical exercise.

Energy for Muscle Contraction

The basic energy sources for muscles, ATP (adenosine triphosphate) and PC (phosphocreatine), are produced by the body. A muscle will expend its entire store of these compounds in only a few seconds of exercise. Depending on the type and duration of exercise, the ATP in the muscles is resupplied either by carbohydrates (glucose in blood or glycogen in the muscle or liver) or stored fats. The duration and intensity of exercise will determine what type of fuel the muscle will use for energy. Exercises lasting one to two minutes are fueled by the anaerobic process (without oxygen) since little oxygen is available during this period of time. Sprinting, weight lifting and jumping are examples of anaerobic activities. If the exercise continues past two minutes, the body is required to draw upon oxygen (aerobic). The oxygen system can utilize both glycogen and fats for fuel for the production of ATP. Activities that are low to moderate in intensity and of long duration such as jogging, long-distance swimming, and cross-country skiing use fat as their primary energy source.

Diets

The world is full of hundreds of various diets. However, no matter which diets are used (except for a specific medical problem) each diet should be judged by the following criteria:

Diet Rating

1. Does the diet provide a reasonable number of kcalories (kcal), enough to maintain weight but not an excess; and if a reduction diet, not fewer than 1200 kcal for the average-size person?
2. Does it provide enough, but not too much protein, at least the recommended intake or RDA (Recommended Daily Allowance), but not more than twice as much?
3. Does it provide enough fat for satiety, but not so much fat as to exceed current recommendations, between twenty and thirty-five percent of the kcal from fat?
4. Does it provide enough carbohydrates to spare protein and prevent ketosis, 100 grams of carbohydrate for the average-size person? Is it mostly complex carbohydrate, not more than twenty percent of the kcal as concentrated sugar?
5. Does it offer a balanced assortment of vitamins and minerals from whole food sources in all four food groups (milk and milk products; meat, fish, poultry, and eggs; legumes, fruits, and vegetables; and grains)?
6. Does it offer variety, in that different foods can be selected each day?
7. Does it consist of ordinary foods that are available locally and at prices people normally pay?

Source: adapted from E. N. Whitney, M.A. Boyle, Understanding Nutrition, fourth edition, West Publishing Co., St. Paul, MN, 1987.

The following list presents basic nutritional guidelines.

Basic Nutritional Recommendations

1. Increase consumption of fruits and vegetables.
2. Decrease consumption of red and organ meats and increase consumption of poultry and fish. Remember, shrimp and lobster are higher in cholesterol than other fish.
3. Decrease consumption of foods high in fat and substitute polyunsaturated and monosaturated fat for saturated fat. Reduce saturated fat consumption to about ten percent of total energy intake.
4. Substitute skim milk (nonfat milk) for whole milk.
5. Decrease consumption of butterfat, eggs and other sources high in cholesterol. Reduce cholesterol intake to 300 milligrams a day (equivalent of one egg).
6. Decrease consumption of refined foods (cane and beet sugar) and processed foods (corn sugar, syrups, molasses, honey) that are high in sugar content.
7. Increase consumption of complex carbohydrates: grains, breads, cereals, potatoes, corn, and rice.
8. Decrease consumption of salt and foods with a high salt content.

How to Gain Weight

The best way to gain weight is to build muscle mass through careful and consistent physical training. Eat a well balanced and nutritious diet with enough calories in the form of complex carbohydrates to support a weight gain.

How to Lose Weight

Exercise is an integral part of any weight loss program. Approximately 3500 kcalories are contained in one pound of stored fat. If, for example, your food intake for one day is equivalent to 2200 kcalories and you burn up 2200 kcalories in your daily activity you will be in caloric balance, you will not gain or lose weight. However, if you burn up an additional 100 kcalories a day through a vigorous exercise program, bringing your total daily expenditure to 2300 and at the same time still taking in only 2200 kcalories, you will incur a deficit of 100 kcalories a day. If you were to continue this regimen for thirty-five days you would accumulate a total caloric deficit of 3500 kcalories which should be equal to a loss of one pound of fat. A deficit of 200 kcalories a day would result in a loss of one pound of fat in one half that time. Maximum weight loss should not exceed two pounds a week or a 1000 kcalories per day deficit.

Glossary

Adenosine triphosphate (ATP)
An energy-rich chemical compound stored in muscle cells; a source of immediate energy.

Carbohydrates
Chemical compounds containing carbon, hydrogen and oxygen; examples are sugars and starches, major sources of energy.

Fats
Food stuffs containing glycerol and fatty acids.

Ketosis
The development of ketone bodies and acidosis (disruption of the acid/base balance) due to improper breakdown of fats.

Kilocalories
The amount of energy required to raise one kilogram of water one degree centigrade.

Minerals
Inorganic compounds some of which are nutrients vital to body function. Examples include phosphorus, calcium, potassium, sodium, iron, and iodine.

Phosphocreatine
A chemical that can donate its phosphate to form ATP in the muscle.

Protein
Organic material that regulates body processes and builds and repairs body tissue.

Vitamins
Organic compounds that regulate a number of body processes and that are used in the metabolism of carbohydrates.

Drugs

15

Objectives

After studying this chapter you should be able to:

1. Describe the present state of drug use in strength training programs.
2. Describe anabolic steroids and their physiological effect on the body.
3. Describe the American College of Sports Medicine position statement on anabolic-androgenic steroids in sport.
4. Describe the effects of amphetamines.
5. Describe the effects of growth hormones.
6. Describe the effects of cocaine.
7. Describe the effects of caffeine.

The use of drugs by professional and amateur athletes to improve performance is prevalent at all competitive levels. Athletes have always looked for that "extra edge" that will give them the advantage over their opponent. With only hundredths of seconds, or a few inches separating the winner from the also-ran, it is not surprising that drugs, thought to increase performance, find wide acceptance. Both male and female competitive athletes are presently using a wide range of pharmacological agents in the belief that it will increase their strength, endurance, speed, power, and skill. One of the most unfortunate aspects of the use of drugs is that many athletes appear to be willing to court major health risks in order to be competitive. They believe they must resort to the use of drugs.

Anabolic Steroids

Anabolic steroids are synthetic hormones and close relatives of testosterone, the male hormone. This hormone has had its chemical structure altered so that the androgenic or masculinizing effect has been reduced and its anabolic protein producing characteristics enhanced in order to promote muscle growth. There is also speculation that small residual androgenic effects increase performance by making the athletes more aggressive and competitive, resulting in an increased intensity of training motivation. Steroids have been used frequently in medical practice for malnutrition, infection, skeletal disorders, some cancers, and growth prob-

Table 15.1   Side Effects That Have Been Observed in Those Using Anabolic Steroids

Males

Liver damage

Impaired thyroid and pituitary function

Impaired cardiovascular function

Increased blood pressure

Prostate gland disorders

Acne, skin rash

Atrophied testes

Increased aggressiveness

Changes in libido

Gastro-intestinal changes

Increased muscle cramps and spasms

Gynecomastia—development of breast-like tissue

Headaches, dizziness, nose bleeds

Females—These effects are in addition to those observed in males.

Deepening voice

Increase in facial/body hair

Acne

Clitoral enlargement

Menstrual irregulation

Increased fibrous (collagen) content of body

lems. Anabolic steroids promote anabolism (muscle growth) by increasing nitrogen retention. They may convert a mildly negative nitrogen balance to a positive one, depending on adequate protein and caloric intake. They may build lean body mass and increase strength in individuals who are intensively training in heavy resistance (weight lifting) activities. They do not directly improve performance in aerobic activities such as long-distance running, skiing or swimming.

The real possibility of harmful side effects greatly outweighs the questionable increases in performance. Table 15.1 outlines the possible side effects of anabolic steroid use in males and females.

Anabolic-androgenic steroids have been associated with adverse effects on the liver, cardiovascular system, reproductive function and psychological status. Steroids that are alkalated at the 17-carbon position (most all oral forms) are specially dangerous because of the strong link between this chemical structure and liver disfunction. There are also additional side effects in women and children. Some are irreversible.

The American College of Sports Medicine Position Statement on Anabolic-Androgenic Steroids in Sports

It is the position of the American College of Sports Medicine that:

1. Anabolic-androgenic steroids in the presence of an adequate diet can contribute to increases in body weight, often in the lean mass compartment.
2. The gains in muscular strength achieved through high-intensity exercise and proper diet can occur by the increased use of anabolic-androgenic steroids in some individuals.
3. Anabolic-androgenic steroids do not increase aerobic power or capacity for muscular exercise.
4. Anabolic-androgenic steroids have been associated with adverse effects on the liver, cardiovascular system, and psychologic status in therapeutic trials and in limited research on athletes. Until further research is completed, the potential hazards of the use of the anabolic-androgenic steroids in athletes must include those found in therapeutic trials.
5. The use of anabolic-androgenic steroids by athletes is contrary to the rules and ethical principles of athletic competition as set forth by many of the sports governing bodies. The American College of Sports Medicine supports these ethical principles and deplores the use of anabolic-androgenic steroids by athletes.

Amphetamines

Amphetamines are a group of drugs that stimulate the central nervous system of the body. They generally cause a rise in blood pressure, cardiac output, blood sugar, breathing rate and metabolism. Athletes take amphetamines in hopes that the increased arousal level and depression of the sensation of muscle fatigue will enable them to maintain higher performance levels for longer periods of time. There is very little scientific evidence that amphetamines improve speed, performance, or increase endurance. Most of the studies report that the drugs have very little effect. Some athletes use amphetamines to "get them up" for competition or psychologically ready to compete. This practice may require the athlete to resort to the use of barbiturates to enable them to come down from the amphetamine high in order to sleep. The result is a dangerous stimulant to depressant combination. One of the dangers of taking amphetamines during exercise is that the individual may overstress the body with possible damage to the heart. Other major risks are psychological dependence and the possibility of circulatory collapse.

Caffeine

There is some recent evidence that caffeine may in some circumstances increase endurance in moderately strenuous activity. Caffeine facilitates the use of fat as a fuel, and increases the permeability of the muscle cell to calcium, resulting in a more efficient contraction and the sparing of glycogen in the muscles. Caffeine may also have a psychostimulating effect, causing the athlete to feel that the exercise was easier. The adverse effects of using caffeine are that some individuals encounter an allergic response, cardiac arrythmias, headaches, insomnia, irritability, and a diuretic effect.

Growth Hormones

There is a major concern that growth hormones (somatotrophic hormone) will replace anabolic steroids as the new high-tech drug. Growth hormone is produced by the pituitary gland in the brain. One of its functions is to stimulate and control the tissue building process of normal growth and development. It is used medically to treat children with retarded growth syndrome. With the advancement of bioengineering it will be soon possible to synthetically produce large amounts of this hormone inexpensively. Athletes are attracted to the drug because it increases protein synthesis and fat breakdown and decreases the amount of carbohydrates used by the body. However, its use in adults can lead to symptoms similar to those of acromegaly: enlarged bones of the face, hands and feet, overgrowth of soft tissue, and a most dangerous abnormal enlargement of cardiac tissue. This hormone is most difficult to detect in screening tests because it occurs naturally in the body.

Cocaine

Cocaine is a central nervous system stimulant producing similar effects as caffeine. Cocaine enhances alertness and masks fatigue. It produces a state of excitement, and restlessness. Euphoria, heightened self-confidence, temporary relief of depression, and suppressed appetite all result from cocaine use. As these effects wear off, the user experiences a period of depression, confusion, and dizziness. Small doses slow the heart, but larger amounts stimulate the heart. Blood pressure increases as a result of constricted blood vessels and respiration becomes shallow and rapid. Repeated use of large doses leads to weight loss, insomnia, anxiety, and paranoid delusion. Inhaling and snorting may also result in ulceration of the nasal tissue. Death may occur due to respiratory or cardiac failure.

Glossary

Amphetamines
Group of drugs that stimulate central nervous system.

Anabolic Steroids
Synthetic hormone similar to male hormone testosterone that stimulates increases in muscle mass.

Anabolism
Constructive metabolism.

Androgenic
A stubstance that stimulates male characteristics.

Caffeine
Chemical found in coffee and tea that acts as stimulant on central nervous system.

Cocaine
Central nervous system stimulant derived from coca leaves.

Diuretic
A substance that increases kidney function, secretion of urine, and water loss.

Equipment

16

Objectives

After studying this chapter you should be able to:

1. Describe the use of free weights and barbells in strength training programs.
2. Describe Cybex Knee Extension, Mini-Gym, Universal Machine, Nautilus, CAMII, Hydra Fitness, Polaris, Free Weights, and Power Exercise equipment.

Equipment

The following are the major categories of resistive exercise equipment used to train muscles:

1. Free weights and barbells; this equipment cannot control speed or resistance through the full range of movement yet produces different levels of muscle stress at different points in the range of movement. There is a place in the range of movement, the sticking point, at which the mechanical factors are least favorable and the greatest amount of muscle force is required. In very heavy loads (1 RM) the exercise produces maximum stress at only one point in the range of movement. The advantage is that this type of equipment most closely mimics the action found in ballistic sport skills such as kicking and throwing.
2. Equipment that provides controlled or constant speed and variable resistance (true isokinetic equipment controls speed). This type of equipment, including point 3 and 4, closely mimics sport skills that require tension movements through the range of movement, such as swimming and cycling.
3. Equipment controls a constant and variable resistance by means of a hydraulic device.
4. Equipment where speed is variable and resistance is constant (some CAM devices and concentric-eccentric devices).
5. There is currently no machine whereby muscles contract under conditions of true constant speed and true constant resistance.

Cybex Knee Extension

These are extension test machines which use electric servo-breaking to provide nearly complete accommodating resistance so that muscles shorten at a constant speed and can be maximally loaded throughout the full range of motion. They are used mainly in strength testing, rehabilitation and research.

Mini-Gym

As a greater muscle force is applied, greater frictional forces are produced resulting in a proportional increase in resistance and a steady movement speed. Eccentric contractions, however, cannot be performed with this equipment.

Universal Machine

This multi-station apparatus may use a sliding fulcrum to alter the resistance of weight blocks. It duplicates most free weights exercises.

Nautilus

A cam compensates for the variations in muscular force at different joint angles by changing the lever arm. As a result the muscles exert maximal or near maximal force throughout the full range of motion in both positive and negative phases of muscle contraction.

CAM II

The apparatus uses pneumatic or air resistance by means of compressed air and pneumatic cylinders.

Hydra Fitness

This machine offers accommodating resistance that controls the speed of movement by restricting the speed of movement of hydraulic fluid through a hydraulic cylinder.

Polaris

With this device the weight to be moved is drawn over an oval-shaped plate. The muscles can move through a full range of movement in both positive and negative phases of muscle contraction.

Free Weights

Barbells and dumbbells allow exercise in both positive and negative phases of muscle contraction.

Power Exercise Equipment

These devices are computerized and use artificial intelligence. They coach the individual through his or her workout, giving verbal encouragement and stating when an increase in resistance is needed.

As long as you follow the basic principles of strength training as explained in chapter 3, you may accomplish your goals with any type of equipment. Whatever you enjoy and find gives satisfaction, security, and confidence is appropriate.

Appendix A
Anatomy Chart

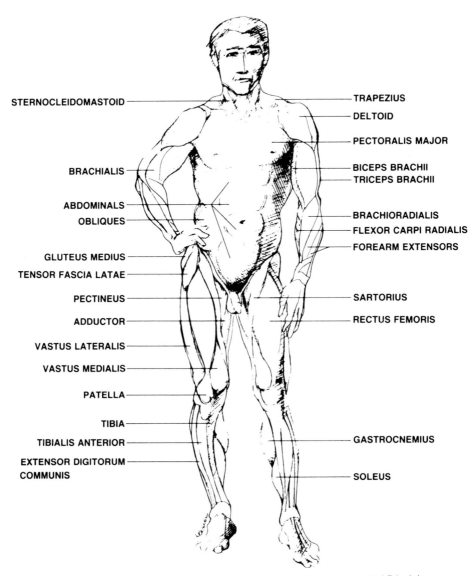

STERNOCLEIDOMASTOID

TRAPEZIUS

DELTOID

PECTORALIS MAJOR

BRACHIALIS

BICEPS BRACHII
TRICEPS BRACHII

ABDOMINALS
OBLIQUES

BRACHIORADIALIS
FLEXOR CARPI RADIALIS
FOREARM EXTENSORS

GLUTEUS MEDIUS
TENSOR FASCIA LATAE

PECTINEUS

SARTORIUS

ADDUCTOR

RECTUS FEMORIS

VASTUS LATERALIS

VASTUS MEDIALIS

PATELLA

TIBIA

TIBIALIS ANTERIOR

GASTROCNEMIUS

EXTENSOR DIGITORUM
COMMUNIS

SOLEUS

Muscles of the Body: Front. From Wayne L. Westcott, Strength Fitness: Physiological Principles and Training Techniques. Copyright © 1989 Wm. C. Brown Publishers, Dubuque, Iowa. All Rights Reserved. Reprinted by permission.

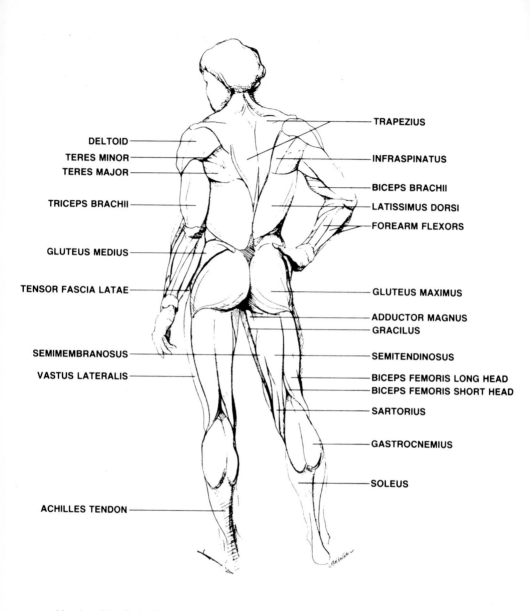

DELTOID
TERES MINOR
TERES MAJOR
TRICEPS BRACHII
GLUTEUS MEDIUS
TENSOR FASCIA LATAE
SEMIMEMBRANOSUS
VASTUS LATERALIS
ACHILLES TENDON

TRAPEZIUS
INFRASPINATUS
BICEPS BRACHII
LATISSIMUS DORSI
FOREARM FLEXORS
GLUTEUS MAXIMUS
ADDUCTOR MAGNUS
GRACILUS
SEMITENDINOSUS
BICEPS FEMORIS LONG HEAD
BICEPS FEMORIS SHORT HEAD
SARTORIUS
GASTROCNEMIUS
SOLEUS

Muscles of the Body: Back. From Wayne L. Westcott, Strength Fitness: Physiological Principles and Training Techniques. Copyright © 1989 Wm. C. Brown Publishers, Dubuque, Iowa. All Rights Reserved. Reprinted by permission.

Appendix B
Weight Exercises and Major Muscles Involved

Biceps - Barbell curls, dumbbell curls, pull-ups, reverse curls.

Triceps - French curls, tricep extensor (standing or lat machine). Bar - dips, military press, bench press, pull-over (bent arm).

Brachialis - Reverse curls, upright rowing.

Deltoids - Military press, behind the neck press, dumbbell press, upright rowing, pull-overs (bent arm), lateral raise (standing), bent rowing.

Flexor carpi - Wrist curls, curls, grip machine.

Pectoralis - Bench press, lateral raise (incline or supine), pull-over and press, lat pull (machine).

Trapezius - Shoulder shrugs, behind the neck press.

Rhomboids - Bent rowing, shoulder shrugs, lat pull (machine).

Latissimus dorsi - Lat pull (machine), bent rowing, dumbbell rowing, pullover (bent arm).

Serratus - Pull-over (bent or straight arm).

Abdominals - Sit-ups (all varieties), scissor kick (incline), leg lifts (hanging), leg pullover (incline).

External obliques - Side bending (dumbbell or barbell), stiff legged side lift.

Erector Spinae - Stiff legged dead lift, dead lift, back hyperextensions.

Gluteus Maximus - Squats, leg press (machine).

Quadriceps - Squats, leg press (machine), knee extension (machine).

Hamstrings - Knee flexions (machine), squats.

Gastrocnemius - Toe raises (leg press machine or standing) and soleus.

Appendix C
Weight Training Activities for Various Sports

Movement	Neck flexion and extension	Shoulder shrug	Military or overhead press	Behind the neck press	Upright rowing	Bent rowing	Lat machine	Triceps extension	Lateral arm raise	Bent-arm pull-over	Biceps curl	Dumbbell curl	Bench press	Incline press	Parallel bar dip	Back hyperextension	Trunk extension	Weighted sit-ups	Hip flexion	Stiff leg dead lift	Knee flexion	Knee extension	Squat	Hack squat	Toe raise
Baseball					x			x	x				x				x	x					x		
Basketball					x		x		x	x			x	x				x			x	x			x
Golf					x						x	x	x	x				x		x			x	x	
Gymnastics			x		x			x	x	x			x		x	x	x								
Football	x	x	x			x							x	x		x		x		x			x	x	
Soccer	x			x							x	x	x	x	x			x		x			x	x	
Rowing					x		x			x			x	x		x	x	x	x				x	x	
Tennis		x	x		x			x	x				x		x					x	x				
Wrestling	x	x					x	x	x				x	x	x	x	x	x					x	x	
Skiing		x			x			x	x				x		x	x		x					x	x	x
Hockey	x	x	x			x		x	x				x		x	x	x						x		
Backstroke		x		x	x	x							x					x			x		x		
Breaststroke			x		x	x		x					x			x		x				x	x		
Butterfly				x	x	x		x					x			x		x				x	x		
Freestyle			x		x	x							x			x	x						x		
Sprinting													x				x	x			x	x	x	x	
Hurdling							x	x			x			x			x				x	x	x	x	
Javelin		x	x					x		x			x					x			x	x	x	x	
Long jump								x		x			x							x		x	x		
Distance running			x					x			x	x						x		x			x		x
Pole vault	x		x						x	x	x	x	x		x			x					x		
High jump										x	x		x	x				x					x	x	x
Discus and Shot Put		x						x			x	x	x				x	x					x	x	

Adapted from J. P. O'Shea, Scientific Principles and Methods of Strength Fitness. 1976. 2d. ed. McGraw-Hill Publishing Company.

Appendix D
Weight Training Standards for College Age Males

The far right column indicates the percentile ranking of each weight lifted. For example, a bench press of 125 lbs for an individual who weighs between 130–139 lbs would correspond to the fifty percentile. In other words fifty percent of the individuals in the weight category pressed over 125 lbs and the remaining fifty percent pressed less than 125 lbs—standard based on 2,500 male college students.

Body Weight Class 120–129 lbs.

Sit-Up	Curl	Upright rowing	Over-Head Press	Bench Press	Squat	Bent-Over Rowing	%
70	107.5	120	155	170	255	185	100
65	105	117.5	150	165	245	182.5	99.9
62.5	102.5	115	145	160	235	180	99.8
60	100	112.5	140	155	225	170	99.4
57.5	97.5	110	135	150	220	165	98.4
55	95	107.5	130	145	210	157.5	96.2
52.5	92.5	105	125	140	200	150	90.3
50	90	102.5	120	135	190	140	84.2
45	85	100	115	130	180	135	75.8
42.5	82.5	95	110	125	170	127.5	64.0
40	80	90	105	120	160	120	50.0
37.5	77.5	85	100	115	150	112.5	36.0
35	75	80	95	110	140	105	24.2
30	70	77.5	90	105	130	100	15.8
27.5	67.5	75	85	100	120	90	11.6
25	65	72.5	80	95	110	95	9.7
22.5	62.5	70	75	90	100	80	3.8
20	60	68.5	70	85	95	75	1.6
17.5	57.5	65	65	80	85	70	.2
15	55	62.5	60	75	75	65	.1
12.5	52.5	60	55	70	65	60	0

Body Weight Class 130–139 lbs.

Sit-Up	Curl	Upright Rowing	Over-Head Press	Bench Press	Squat	Bent-Over Rowing	%
70	112.5	125	165	175	265	150	100
65	110	122.5	160	170	255	145	99.9
62.5	107.5	120	155	165	245	142.5	99.8
60	105	117.5	150	160	235	140	99.4
57.5	102.5	115	145	155	230	135	98.4
55	100	112.5	140	150	220	130	96.2
52.5	97.5	110	135	145	210	125	90.3
50	95	107.5	130	140	200	120	84.2
45	90	105	125	135	190	117.5	75.8
42.5	87.5	100	120	130	180	115	64.0
40	85	95	115	125	170	110	50.0
37.5	82.5	92.5	110	120	160	105	36.0
35	80	90	105	115	150	102.5	24.2
30	75	85	100	110	140	100	15.8
27.5	72.5	80	95	105	130	95	11.6
25	70	77.5	90	100	120	90	9.7
22.5	67.5	75	85	95	110	85	3.8
20	65	72.5	80	90	105	80	1.6
17.5	60	70	75	85	95	75	.2
15	57.5	67.5	70	80	85	70	.1
12.5	55	65	65	75	80	65	0

Body Weight Class 140–149 lbs.

Sit-Up	Curl	Upright Rowing	Over-Head Press	Bench Press	Squat	Bent-Over Rowing	%
70	117.5	130	170	185	275	205	100
65	115	127.5	165	180	270	197.5	99.9
62.5	112.5	125	160	175	260	190	99.8
60	110	122.5	155	170	250	180	99.4
57.5	107.5	120	150	165	240	175	98.4
55	105	117.5	145	160	230	167.5	96.2
52.5	102.5	115	140	155	220	160	90.3
50	100	112.5	135	150	210	150	84.2
45	95	110	130	145	200	145	75.8
42.5	92.5	107.5	125	140	190	137.5	64.0
40	90	105	120	135	180	130	50.0
37.5	87.5	102.5	115	130	170	122.5	36.0
35	85	100	110	125	160	115	24.2
30	82.5	95	105	120	150	110	15.8
27.5	80	90	100	115	140	100	11.6
25	77.5	87.5	95	110	130	95	9.7
22.5	75	85	90	105	120	90	3.8
20	72.5	82.5	85	100	115	85	1.6
17.5	70	80	80	95	105	80	.2
15	67.5	77.5	75	90	100	75	.1
12.5	65	75	70	85	95	70	0

Body Weight Class 150–159 lbs.

Sit-Up	Curl	Upright Rowing	Over-Head press	Bench Press	Squat	Bent-Over Rowing	%
75	122.5	135	175	195	290	210	100
72.5	120	132.5	170	190	285	202.5	99.9
70	117.5	130	165	185	275	195	99.8
65	115	127.5	160	180	267	185	99.4
62.5	112.5	125	155	175	255	180	98.4
60	110	122.5	150	170	245	172.5	96.2
57.5	107.5	120	145	165	235	165	90.3
55	105	117.5	140	160	225	155	84.2
50	100	115	135	155	215	150	75.8
47.5	97.5	112.5	130	150	205	142.5	64.0
45	95	110	125	145	195	135	50.0
42.5	92.5	107.5	120	140	185	127.5	36.0
40	90	105	115	135	175	120	24.2
35	85	102.5	110	130	165	115	15.8
32.5	82.5	100	105	125	155	105	11.6
30	80.5	97.5	100	120	145	100	9.7
27.5	77.5	95	92.5	115	135	95	3.8
25	75	92.5	90	110	125	90	1.6
20	72.5	90	85	105	120	85	.2
17.5	70	87.5	80	100	115	80	.1
15	67.5	85	75	95	110	75	0

Body Weight Class 160–169 lbs.

Sit-Up	Curl	Upright Rowing	Over-Head Press	Bench Press	Squat	Bent-Over Rowing	%
75	125	140	180	205	305	215	100
72.5	122.5	137.5	175	200	300	207.5	99.9
70	120	135	170	195	290	200	99.8
65	117.5	132.5	165	190	280	190	99.4
62.5	115	130	160	185	270	185	98.4
60	112.5	127.5	155	180	260	177.5	96.2
57.5	110	125	150	175	250	170	90.3
55	107.5	122.5	145	170	240	160	84.2
50	105	120	140	165	230	155	75.8
47.5	102.5	117.5	135	160	220	147.5	64.0
45	100	115	130	155	210	140	50.0
42.5	97.5	112.5	125	150	200	132.5	36.0
40	95	110	120	145	190	125	24.2
35	92.5	107.5	115	140	180	120	15.8
32.5	90	105	110	135	170	110	11.6
30	87.5	102.5	105	130	160	105	9.7
27.5	85	100	100	125	150	100	3.8
25	82.5	97.5	95	120	140	95	1.6
20	80	95	90	115	135	90	.2
17.5	77.5	92.5	85	110	130	85	.1
15	75	90	80	105	125	80	0

Body Weight Class 170–179 lbs.

Sit-Up	Curl	Upright Rowing	Over-Head Press	Bench Press	Squat	Bent-Over Rowing	%
75	124	145	185	215	315	220	100
72.5	122.5	142.5	180	210	310	212.5	99.9
70	120	140	175	205	300	205	99.8
65	117.5	137.5	170	200	290	195	99.4
62.5	115	135	165	195	280	190	98.4
60	112.5	132.5	160	190	270	182.5	96.2
57.5	110	130	155	185	260	175	90.3
55	107.5	127.5	150	180	250	165	84.2
50	105	125	145	175	240	160	75.8
47.5	102.5	122.5	140	170	235	152.5	64.0
45	100	120	135	165	225	145	50.0
42.5	97.5	117.5	130	160	215	137.5	36.0
40	95	115	125	155	205	130	24.2
35	92.5	112.5	120	150	195	125	15.8
30.5	90.5	110	115	145	185	115	11.6
30	87.5	107.5	110	140	175	110	9.7
27.5	85	105	105	135	165	105	3.8
25	82.5	102.5	100	130	155	100	1.6
20	80	100	95	125	150	95	.2
17.5	77.5	97.5	90	120	145	90	.1
15	75	95	85	115	140	85	0

Body Weight Class 180–189 lbs.

Sit-Up	Curl	Upright Rowing	Over-Head Press	Bench Press	Squat	Bent-Over Rowing	%
75	130	150	190	225	325	225	100
72.5	127.5	147.5	185	220	320	217.5	99.9
70	125	145	180	215	310	210	99.8
65	122.5	142.5	175	210	305	200	99.4
62.5	120	140	170	205	295	195	98.4
60	117.5	137.5	165	200	285	187.5	96.2
57.5	115	135	160	195	275	180	90.3
55	112.5	132.5	155	190	265	170	84.2
50	110	130	150	185	255	165	75.8
47.5	107.5	127.5	145	180	250	157.5	64.0
45	105	125	140	175	240	150	50.0
42.5	102.5	122.5	135	170	230	142.5	36.0
40	100	120	130	165	220	135	24.2
35	97.5	117.5	125	160	210	130	15.8
32.5	95	115	120	155	200	120	11.6
30	92.5	112.5	115	150	190	115	9.7
27.5	90	110	110	145	180	110	3.8
25	87.5	107.5	105	140	170	105	1.6
20	85	105	100	135	165	100	.2
17.5	82.5	102.5	95	130	155	95	.1
15	80	100	90	125	150	90	0

Body Weight Class 190 lbs. +

Sit-Up	Curl	Upright Rowing	Over-Head Press	Bench Press	Squat	Bent-Over Rowing	%
75	135	155	195	235	335	230	100
72.5	132.5	152.5	190	230	330	222.5	99.9
70	130	150	185	225	320	215	99.8
65	127.5	147.5	180	220	315	205	99.4
62.5	125	145	175	215	305	200	98.4
60	122.5	142.5	170	210	295	192.5	96.2
57.5	120	140	165	205	285	180	90.3
55	117.5	137.5	160	200	275	175	84.2
50	115	135	155	195	265	170	75.8
47.5	112.5	132.5	150	190	260	162.5	64.0
45	110	130	145	185	250	155	50.0
42.5	107.5	127.5	140	180	240	147.5	36.0
40	105	125	135	175	230	140	24.2
35	102.5	122.5	130	170	220	135	15.8
32.5	100	120	125	165	210	125	11.6
30	97.5	117.5	120	160	200	120	9.7
27.5	95	115	115	155	190	115	3.8
25	92.5	112.5	110	150	180	110	1.6
20	90	110	105	145	175	105	.2
17.5	87.5	107.5	100	140	165	100	.1
15	85	105	95	135	155	95	0

Source: Berger, R. A. Weight Training Standards for Adult Males (unpublished), Biokinetics Research Laboratory, Temple University, Philadelphia, PA.

Appendix E
Universal Super Circuit

On the following two pages is a new high intensity program for athletes. It is designed to develop all four elements of fitness: strength, muscular endurance, cardiorespiratory endurance and flexibility. It can be used for preseason conditioning and is a quick way to get a thorough and balanced workout.

Important Notes:

Be sure to consult your physician and obtain prior approval before engaging in this or any other strenuous training program.
Be sure to begin each exercise period by warming up and stretching to warm up the heart as well as the muscles.
    The program shown on the following pages is meant to be performed on twelve Universal single-station machines, but can also be performed on a multi-station machine.
    This program consists of alternating upper and lower body exercises: the aim is to reach target heart rate. See chapter 12.
    Key to program: You do thirty seconds of aerobic conditioning (running in place, exercycle, jump rope, etc.) between each exercise station.

Procedures

1. How many reps? Fifteen to twenty
2. How many sets? One at each station
3. How many circuits? Three to five
4. How long at each station? Maximum thirty seconds
5. Intervals between stations. Thirty seconds of aerobic conditioning (run in place, jump rope, exercycle, etc.)
6. How much weight? forty to fifty percent maximum for average person, fifty to seventy percent for conditioned athlete
7. How to determine working weight? Find out your maximum for one lift, take percent of that for working weight. Reevaluate every six to eight weeks.
8. Breathing: Exhale as weight goes up, inhale as weight comes down

UNIVERSAL AEROBIC

At each of the numbered stations do one set of 15-20 reps. Maximum 30 seconds at each station. *In between* each station, do 30 seconds of aerobic conditioning. Do the circuit 3-5 times.

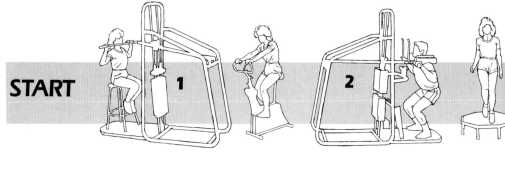

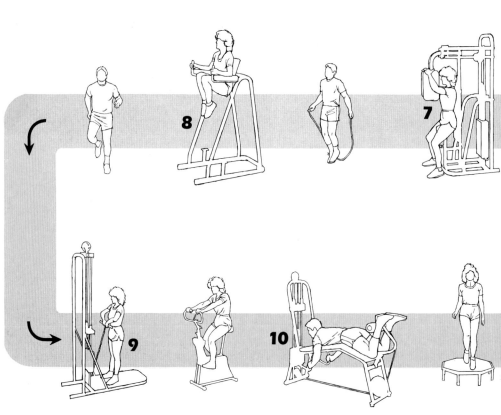

Pearl, Bill, and Moran, Gary. Getting Stronger. Shelter Publications. Bolinas, Calif., 1986.

SUPER CIRCUIT

3

4

6

5

11

12

FINISH

9. Intensity: Make your muscles contract explosively throughout the full range of motion to simulate natural resistance of athletic events.
10. Cool-down: Don't head for the showers until pulse, breathing and perspiration are back to normal. Gradually decrease body movement, reversing the way you warmed up.

At each of the numbered stations do one set of fifteen to twenty reps. Maximum thirty seconds at each station. *In between* each station, do thirty seconds of aerobic conditioning. Do the circuit three to five times.

Appendix F
Aerobic Running Program

Table 6.1 Walking/Jogging Program for Cardiovascular Fitness

Fitness category	Starting level
"Very poor" to "poor"	1 to 2
"Average" to "good"	2 to 3
"Very good" to "excellent"	4 to 5
"Superior"	5 to 7

Level	Exercise	Heart rate training effect level (intensity)	Frequency	Duration
1	Walk for 10 to 20 minutes.	60%	3 days	2 to 4 weeks
2	Walk fast for 15 to 20 minutes.	60%	3 days	2 to 4 weeks
3	Jog 100 yards and then walk 300 yards. Repeat four times. Add one repetition for each succeeding exercise session. When you reach eight repetitions, move to level 4. (approximately 30 minutes)	60%	3 days	2 to 3 weeks
4	Jog 200 yards and then walk 200 yards. Repeat four times. Add one repetition for each succeeding exercise session. When you reach eight repetitions, move to level 5. (approximately 28 minutes)	60%	3 to 4 days	2 to 3 weeks
5	Jog 400 yards and then walk 400 yards. Repeat four times. Add one repetition for each succeeding exercise session. When you reach eight repetitions, move to level 6. (approximately 26 minutes)	70%	3 to 4 days	2 to 3 weeks
6	Jog 800 yards and then walk 400 yards. Repeat four times. Add one repetition for every other exercise session. When you reach six repetitions, move to level 7. (approximately 22 minutes)	70%	3 to 5 days	2 to 3 weeks
7	Jog 1,200 yards and then walk 600 yards. Repeat two times. Add one repetition for every other exercise session. When you reach four repetitions, move to level 8. (approximately 22 minutes)	70%	3 to 5 days	2 to 3 weeks
8	Jog 1 mile in 10 minutes and then walk 3 minutes. Then jog 1 mile again in 10 to 12 minutes.	70%	3 to 5 days	2 to 3 weeks
9	Jog 1½ miles in 15 minutes and then walk 6 to 8 minutes. Then jog again 1½ miles in 15 to 18 minutes.	70%	3 to 5 days	2 to 3 weeks
10	Jog 2 miles in 20 minutes.	70%	3 to 5 days	2 to 3 weeks
11	Jog 2 miles in 18 minutes.	70%	3 to 5 days	2 to 3 weeks
12	Jog 2 miles in 16 minutes.	70%	3 to 5 days	2 to 3 weeks
13	Jog 2 miles in 14 minutes.	70%	3 to 5 days	2 to 3 weeks
14	Continue at level 13 to maintain lifetime fitness.			

Source: From *Dynamics of Fitness: A Practical Approach* by George H. McGlynn. Copyright © 1987. Wm. C. Brown Publishers, Dubuque, Iowa.

Appendix G
Weight Training Progress Chart

Weight Training Record Card

Name _____

Class _____

After

Weight	
Right Bicep	
Left Bicep	
Chest Inf.	
Chest Def.	
Abdominal Girth	
Right Thigh	
Left Thigh	
Hip	

Dates		W	R	W	R	W	R	W	R	W	R	W	R	W	R	W	R
Exercises																	
	1																
	2																
	3																
	1																
	2																
	3																
	1																
	2																
	3																
	1																
	2																
	3																
	1																
	2																
	3																
	1																
	2																
	3																
	1																
	2																
	3																

Weight Training Record Card

Name _____

Class _____

Weight	
Right Bicep	
Left Bicep	
Chest Inf.	
Chest Def.	
Abdominal Girth	
Right Thigh	
Left Thigh	
Hip	

Dates																
Exercises		W	R	W	R	W	R	W	R	W	R	W	R	W	R	W	R
	1																
	2																
	3																
	1																
	2																
	3																
	1																
	2																
	3																
	1																
	2																
	3																
	1																
	2																
	3																
	1																
	2																
	3																
	1																
	2																
	3																

Appendix H
Suggested Readings

Motivation

Garfield, Charles A., and Hal Z. Bennett. *Peak Performance—Mental Training Techniques of the World's Greatest Athletes*. Los Angeles, Ca: J. P. Tarcher, Inc., 1984.

Jerome, John. *Staying With It*. New York: The Viking Press, 1984.

Suinn, R. M. *Psychology in Sports: Methods and Applications*. Minneapolis, Mn: Burgess, 1980.

Tutko, Thomas A., and Umberto Tosi. *Sports Psyching—Playing Your Best Game All of the Time*. Los Angeles, Ca: J. P. Tartcher, Inc., 1976.

Williams, Jean M. *Applied Sports Psychology*. Palo Alto, Ca.: Mayfield Press, 1986.

Nutrition and Weight Control

Briggs, George M., and Doris H. Calloway. *Bogert's Nutrition and Physical Fitness*. Philadelphia: Saunders, 1979.

Brody, Jane. *Jane Brody's Nutrition Book*. New York: Norton, 1981.

Guthrie, Helen. *Introductory Nutrition*. St. Louis: C. V. Mosby, 1983.

Katch, Frank I., and William D. McArdle. *Nutrition, Weight Control and Exercise*. Boston: Houghton Mifflin, 1977.

Whitney, Eleanor N., and Corinne B. Bataldo. *Understanding Normal and Clinical Nutrition*. St. Paul: West, 1983.

Physical Fitness and Health

Allsen, Phillip E., Joyce M. Harrison, and Barbara Vance. *Fitness for Life, 3d.ed.* Dubuque, Iowa: Wm. C. Brown Publishers, 1984.

Cooper, Kenneth. *Aerobics Program for Total Well Being*. New York: Evans, 1982.

Corbin, Charles and Ruth Lindsy. *Concepts of Physical Fitness with Laboratory. 5th ed.* Dubuque, Iowa: Wm. C. Brown Publishers, 1985.

Di Gennaro, Joseph. *The New Physical Fitness: Exercise for Every Body*. Englewood, Colo.: Morton, 1983.

Dintiman, George B., Stephan E. Stone, Jude C. Pennington, and Robert G. Davis. *Discovering Lifetime Fitness*. St. Paul: West, 1984.

Falls, Arnold B., Ann M. Baylor, and Rud K. Dishman. *Essentials of Fitness*. Philadelphia: Saunders, 1980.

Getchell, Bud. *Physical Fitness, A Way of Life. 3d. ed.* New York: Wiley, 1983.

Marley, William. *Health and Physical Fitness*. Philadelphia: Saunders, 1982.

McGlynn, George H. *Dynamics of Fitness/A Practical Approach*. Dubuque, Iowa: Wm. C. Brown Publishers, 1987.

Pollock, Michael, Jack H. Wilmore, and Samuel M. Fox. *Exercise in Health and Disease*. Philadelphia: Saunders, 1984.

Rosensweig, S. *Sports Fitness for Women*. New York: Harper & Row, 1982.

Wilmore, Jack. *Sensible Fitness*. Leisure Press, 1986.

Physiology of Exercise

Brooks, George A., and Thomas D. Fahey. *Exercise Physiology*. New York: John Wiley & Sons, 1984.

Devries, Herbert A. *Physiology of Exercise for Physical Education and Athletics. 3d ed.* Philadelphia: Saunders, 1980.

Fox, E. L. *Sports Physiology*. Philadelphia: Saunders, 1979.

Lamb, David R. *Physiology of Exercise*. New York: Macmillan, 1984.

Shaver, Larry G. *Essentials of Exercise Physiology*. Minneapolis: Burgess, 1981.

Wilmore, Jack H. *Training for Sport and Activity, The Physiological Basis of Conditioning. 2d ed.* Boston: Allyn & Bacon, 1982.

Wells, C. L. *Women, Sport and Performance, A Physiological Perspective*. Champaign, Ill.: Human Kinetics Publisher, 1985.

Strength and Muscle Development

Bass, Charles. *Ripped—The Sensible Way to Achieve Ultimate Muscularity*. Albuquerque, NM.: Ripped Enterprises, 1980.

Darden, Ellington. *The Nautilus Book*. Chicago: Contemporary Books, 1982.

Darden, Ellington. *The Nautilus Woman*. New York: Simon & Schuster, 1983.

Fox, E. L., and D. K. Mathews. *Interval Training, Conditioning for Sport and General Fitness*. Philadelphia: Saunders, 1974.

Gaines, Charles, and George Butler. *Pumping Iron II: The Unprecedented Woman*. New York: Simon & Schuster, 1984.

Hatfield, Frederick C. *The Complete Guide To Power Training*. New Orleans. Fitness Systems, 1983, Lakewood Ca.: Sports Conditioning Services, 5542 South Street, 90713.

Jarrell, Steve. *Working Out with Weights*. New York: Anco, 1982.

Kennedy, Robert. *Reps!—Building Massive Muscle!* New York: Sterling Publishing Co., Inc., 1985.

Kirkley, George W. *Weight Lifting and Weight Training*. New York: Anco, 1982.

Lance, Kathryn. *Getting Strong—A Woman's Guide to Realizing Her Physical Potential*. New York: The Bobbs-Merrill Co., Inc., 1978.

Leon, Edie. *Complete Woman Weight Training Guide*. Mountain View, Ca.: Anderson World, 1976.

Lyon, Lisa, and Douglas Kent Hall. *Lisa Lyon's Body Magic.* New York: Bantam Books, 1981.

O'Shea, J. P. *Scientific Principles and Methods of Strength Fitness.* Reading, Mass.: Addison-Wesley, 1979.

Pearl, Bill, and Gary Moran. *Getting Stronger.* Bolinas, Ca.: Shelter, 1986.

Pirie, Lynne, and Bill Reynolds. *Getting Built—A Women's Body Building Program for Strength, Beauty and Fitness.* New York: Warner Books, 1984.

Sobey, Edwin. *Strength Training Book.* Mountain View, Ca.: Anderson World, 1981.

Todd, Jan, and Terry Todd. *Lift Your Way to Youthful Fitness—The Comprehensive Guide to Weight Training.* Boston: Little Brown & Co., 1985.

Webster, David. *Body Building—An Illustrated History.* New York: Arco Publishing, Inc., 1979.

Westcott, Wayne. *Strength Fitness Physiological Principles and Training Techniques.* Boston: Allyn & Bacon, 1983.

Wright, James E. *Anabolic Steroids and Sports.* Natick, Ma: Sports Science Consultants, 1978.

Credits

Photographs: George H. McGlynn and Gary T. Moran
Models: Barbara Gaenslen and George C. McGlynn
Photo Reproduction: Agfa Gevaert
Location: Mariner Square Athletic Club
        2227 Mariner Square Loop
        Alameda, CA 94501

Index